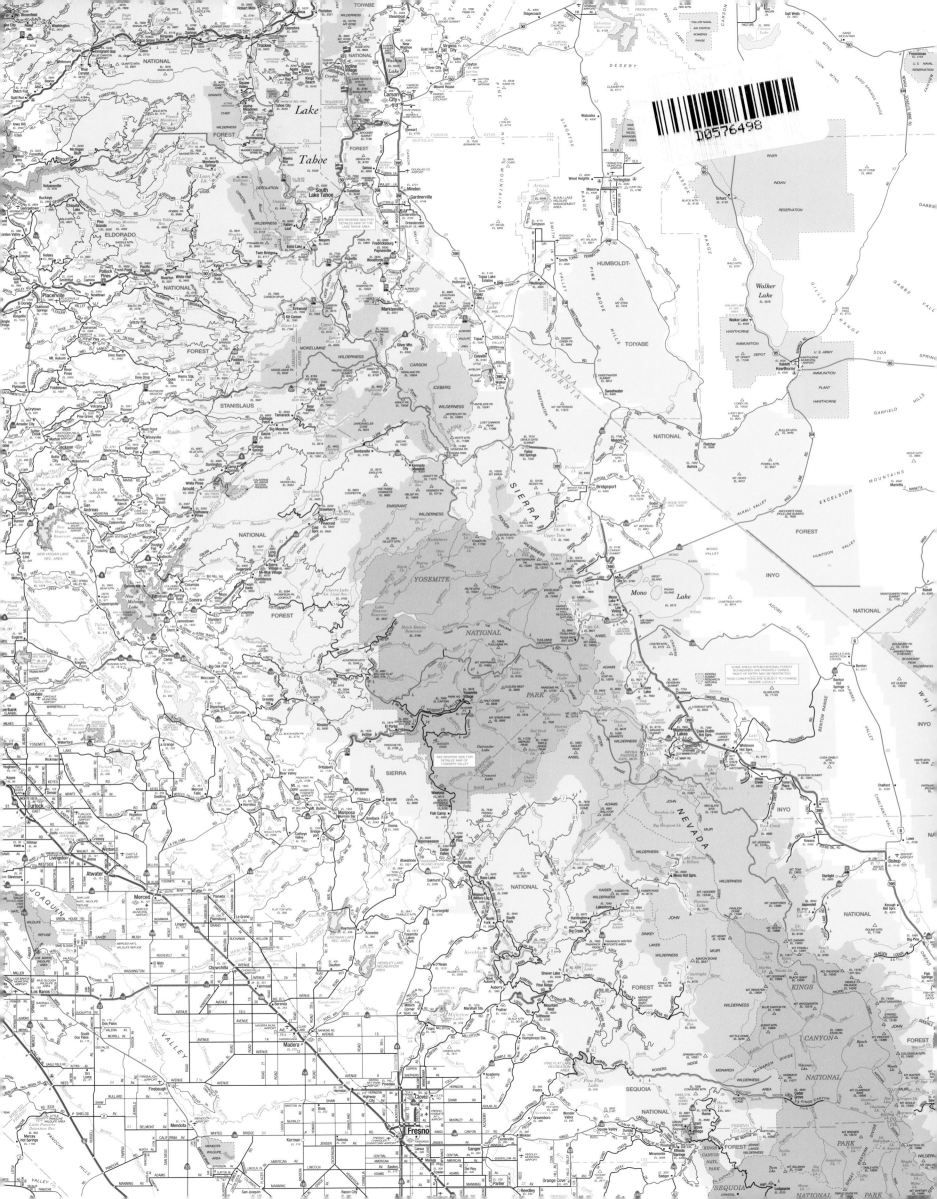

THE SPIRIT OF THE ROAD

ONE HUNDRED YEARS
OF THE **CALIFORNIA STATE**
AUTOMOBILE ASSOCIATION

THE SPIRIT OF THE ROAD

ONE HUNDRED YEARS OF THE CALIFORNIA STATE AUTOMOBILE ASSOCIATION

BY TOM TURNER AND JOHN SPARKS
WITH JOHN GOEPEL AND ALISON MOORE

A WELCOME BOOK

VIA

BOOKS

Preface

At the turn of the last century, there were fewer than two million people in California. There were more oranges than people, and the West still meant ranches, not ranch houses.

Yet even in this rural stage, the land held more than its share of dreamers, people who had come west in search of gold, or new land, or a fresh start. Over the course of the twentieth century, those dreamers, the West's natural abundance, its climate, and world events combined to transform California from a slice of the American social, political, and economic landscape into a global force, Utah into a world-wide destination for vacationers, and Nevada into the home of the world's shiniest city.

The story of California and the West in the twentieth century is a story of people on the move. And that story is one that the California State Automobile Association (CSAA) is uniquely qualified to tell. From the automobile's first appearance in San Francisco, to the present day fascination with the information superhighway, Westerners have trusted CSAA to be their advocate and guide, whether they were on the road, at home, or out exploring the world.

This book tells the story of how the automobile and the personal mobility it provides helped shape a land, a culture, and an organization that grew up to serve its members' needs. From the maps and road signs that helped the first motorists find their way, to the travel and insurance services delivered in one of our offices, over a phone line, or via the Internet, CSAA has been and continues to be "a reassuring comforter to the traveler," providing safety, security, and peace of mind to members and the public.

Buckle your safety belt and join us for a quick history tour. It's been an exciting trip so far, and the road ahead is full of promise.

James P. Molinelli
PRESIDENT AND CEO

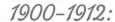

1900–1912:

The Vehicle of Progress

LEFT: Incense Cedar, Ponderosa Pine, and White Fir in Yosemite Valley.

ABOVE: A family takes its Winton for a spin near Santa Ysabel Hot Springs, California, c.1905.

*O*n March 7, 1900, a group of twenty-five self-described San Francisco "automobilists" assembled at the Cliff House to explore the possibilities of the machine that had captured their collective imaginations. With the Pacific Ocean booming at their feet and a new century stretching out before them, the group discussed the future of the horseless carriage and the prospect of forming a club to support the interests of local motorists.

Their host, Cliff House proprietor J. M. Wilkins, was the only one in attendance who actually owned an automobile. At the time, only ten thousand horseless carriages existed in the United States, a mere thirteen of them braving the slopes of San Francisco. But Wilkins could not have been the only one in attendance with

9

ABOVE: The Cliff House. The most ornate of several successive Cliff Houses burned in 1907.

BELOW: Even in California, motoring wasn't all clear skies and smooth roads.

OPPOSITE: A motorist at Yosemite's Glacier Point demonstrates that a car would go where a horse would be too smart to go, c.1900.

an inkling of the impact this new four-wheeled contraption was about to have on the twentieth century. By evening's end, eleven of his twenty-five guests had signed on to form the Auto Club of San Francisco. When they did, the Bay Area received a firm push into the age of the motor vehicle, and the chain of events that would give rise to the California State Automobile Association forged its first solid link.

The club saw itself primarily as a social organization, one dedicated to maximizing the pleasures of motoring. To the minds of club members, the motorcar was a chariot of progress, a vehicle aimed straight at the future. Early motoring expeditions outside the city were adventures into unknown, and largely unpaved, territory. At the turn of the century, less than fifty-thousand miles of America's two-million-mile system of public roads were hard-surfaced. The club's enthusiasm for the horseless carriage was in part a matter of pure faith, as the actual process of driving one was fraught with headaches. Early automobiles teetered constantly on the verge of breakdown, and the puttering racket their engines created was an affront to ears accustomed to the trotting of horses' hooves.

THE SPIRIT OF THE ROAD

ABOVE: Those caught speeding could pay their fines at San Francisco's Hall of Justice on Portsmouth Plaza.

In 1900, resistance to the automobile was fierce. In the eyes of more than a few, this new-fangled, noisy, exhaust-belching contraption was a menace to the well-being of San Francisco and the surrounding cities. Ferrymen refused to transport automobiles across the bay until their tanks had been drained of gasoline. Local governments carved out car-free districts, among them Golden Gate Park and Marin County, where motor vehicles were forbidden to travel. Meanwhile, local police organized what might be called the Dummy Patrol in an effort to discourage the spread of the new invention. Concealed behind roadside bushes, police officers hurled dummies into the path of oncoming autos. Drivers who hit the brakes in time to avoid the dummy were allowed to continue on their way, but those who did not were slapped with a fine or had their driving privileges revoked. The Dummy Patrol may well rank as the first speed trap in the annals of California motoring, and it is undoubtedly the most inspired.

THE SPIRIT OF THE ROAD

Just over a year after the founding of the Auto Club of San Francisco, it became clear that the city's automobilists would need a stronger organization behind them, one willing to roll up its sleeves and take on issues statewide.

On August 19, 1901, seven enthusiasts met at 415 Montgomery Street to form the Automobile Club of California. After electing San Francisco civic leader F. A. Hyde as their president, the club set about staking its claim to the future. While continuing the commitment to the social pleasures of driving, the ACC's Articles of Association make it clear that this group was out for bigger game. Their stated goals included the securing of legislation in favor of the automobilist, the construction and improvement of roads, and the defense of the motor car owner's lawful rights and privileges, this last promising "whenever and wherever such rights and privileges are menaced." The doughty fighting spirit that would inform the creation of the California State Automobile Association six years later was already alive and kicking.

The club's political aims were clear from the outset. At that first meeting on August 19th the directors instructed club member and prominent local attorney H. P. Dimond to draft an ordinance that would standardize the rules of the road for every county in the Bay Area. Putting such an ordinance through would require tenacity and grit, as most local officials still favored traditional forms of horsepower. An anti-auto petition put forward in Marin County summed up the prevailing sentiment when it described theirs as "essentially a horse-keeping and horse-loving county."

BELOW: Looking west on Market Street at Montgomery. The clock tower of the Chronicle building can be seen beyond, 1890s.

AUTOMOBILE
PERMIT

ABOVE: Early in the annals of motoring, drivers did not have automatic access to all places their cars would go. Here is an early driver's license specifically for Golden Gate Park.

BELOW: The car made the outdoors accessible to many more people; the first car to enter Yosemite Valley is thought to have arrived in 1900. This scene took place a few years later.

Indeed, some of the automobile's staunchest opponents were citizens whose livelihoods revolved around the buying and selling of horses. The livery stable owners of San Francisco, for instance, fought to ban "these gasoline-burning machines" from Golden Gate Park because they posed such grave "dangers to the life and limb" of horse-drivers on park lanes and city boulevards.

Club president F. A. Hyde responded to the stable owners' protest with a surprising offer, one he had mailed to every livery stable in the city. The offer, which was reprinted in all the daily newspapers, acknowledged that "the advent of the horse-less carriage has caused more or less inconvenience and sometimes actual danger to those who drive horses on our public streets." This situation could be addressed, however, as "previous experience with bicycles and electric cars has demonstrated the fact that horses will become accustomed to any strange object, whether stationary or moving, if they have seen it a few times." The club offered to post one or more automobiles at some convenient spot in the city, where "the owners of timid horses can bring or send them to be trained." The club received only one response to the offer but, after a meeting time had been arranged, the owner of the timid animal himself proved too timid to show up.

Although the ACC was still predominantly a social club in 1902, Hyde and his fellow club members were aware that the

● *The Automobile Club of San Francisco is formed at San Francisco's famed Cliff House with 11 members.*

● *The Automobile Club of Southern California is founded in Los Angeles.*

● *The Mercedes motorcar is introduced by German automaker Gottlieb Daimler.*

● *William McKinley is reelected president, beating Democrat William Jennings Bryan and Social Democrat Eugene Debs.*

● *The U.S. has 144 miles of concrete roads.*

1901

● *The Automobile Club of San Francisco is renamed the Automobile Club of California. F.A. Hyde is president. The club's first goal is to open Golden Gate Park to automobiles. President McKinley is assassinated; Theodore Roosevelt becomes president.*

1902

● *AAA is founded in Chicago.*

1903

● *The Wright Brothers fly the first powered heavier-than-air craft.*

1904

● *The ACC supports efforts to make the Bay Area's El Camino Real a modern thoroughfare.*

● *Cy Young of the Boston Americans pitches the first perfect game, beating Philadelphia.*

motor vehicle future they saw hovering on the horizon would not come about on its own. Pleasure outings along the back roads of San Mateo County and moonlight runs to the Cliff House made for good sport, but the wheels of true motoring progress were still spinning too slowly. They would gain no real momentum until authorities acknowledged that, as Hyde wrote that year, "the automobile has equal rights on the road with any other vehicle, and … any law which discriminates against the automobile is unconstitutional." By 1903, the club was already roughing out the shape of things to come when it resolved that "a boulevard should be built around the Bay from San Francisco to San Jose and to Oakland."

ABOVE: A 1910 Buick in Alum Rock Park, San Jose, California.

It went like this, the scholars say. First came the wheel, then the axle, then the two-wheeled vehicle drawn by oxen, then the four-wheeled cart and wagon pulled by a team, and finally, the road. It all began at least five thousand years ago in the Middle East. From there, wheeled vehicles moved outward with due deliberation, reaching Denmark a mere 2,500 years later. There is some debate about whether there was spontaneous invention of wheeled vehicles in more than one place, but that need not concern us here. We do know that before 2000 B.C., the streets of Babylon were paved

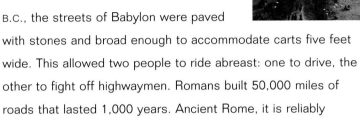

with stones and broad enough to accommodate carts five feet wide. This allowed two people to ride abreast: one to drive, the other to fight off highwaymen. Romans built 50,000 miles of roads that lasted 1,000 years. Ancient Rome, it is reliably reported, had traffic jams.

BUILDING ROADS

Roads began to be developed in the United States in the eighteenth century, but the process stalled with the expansion of the railroads, which dominated until the twentieth century, when the gasoline-powered motorcar took over for good.

When the Automobile Club of California got down to the business of writing purposes and bylaws in 1901, one of the most important was "to promote and encourage in all ways the construction and maintenance of good roads and the improvement of existing highways. . . ."

The need was clear; there were few roads at the time in California that an auto could travel safely. "A drive off a city thoroughfare was an adventure into the unknown," according to *Service First*, a CSAA history published at midcentury. "Motoring was a sufficiently trying experience without bad roads to contend with, for few vehicles had tops, fenders, windshields, or lights. The weak fabric tires took a beating from the rough going, blowouts were frequent, and most motorists didn't venture more than a few miles away from home without taking two to four spares."

In those early days when the ACC gave way to CSAA, "good roads became the prime objective," shown as early as 1903, when the club hierarchy declared that a boulevard should be constructed around the bay from San Francisco to San Jose and Oakland.

As automobile ownership became more commonplace and people began using cars and trucks for commerce as well as for pleasure, it became clear road building would have to be a major responsibility of government, and CSAA began actively campaigning for bond measures to pay for the work. A series of such bonds was offered to the voters and approved. At the same time, CSAA and other clubs put pressure on Washington and, in 1916, a law was passed setting up the framework for a system of federal highways—the Federal Highway Road Act.

ABOVE LEFT AND ABOVE: San Francisco's Ocean Beach before and after the Great Highway was built. With its construction, the Cliff House, Playland, and San Francisco's biggest beach all became easily accessible to anyone with a car.

In 1912, when CSAA director-to-be Burton Towne broke ground on El Camino Real, it was the start of what would become the state highway system we know today. When the system was formally launched in the twenties, planners envisioned two north-south highways, one along the coast, the other through the Central Valley, with trunk lines connecting each county seat to the main arteries. The entire system was expected to cover five thousand miles. When a recalculation was made in 1959 based on projections of number of cars, miles driven, and so forth, the estimate for the total system came out to 12,500 miles, the best engineered and most convenient highway system in the world.

The political tides began to shift in the club's favor in 1905, a year that saw two significant advancements for the motoring cause. The first played itself out on the Mount Hamilton Road to Lick Observatory, a stretch of ground the county of Santa Clara had declared off-limits for cars. Dr. W. W. Campbell, head of the observatory, asked the Automobile Club to put its mettle where its mouth was and do something about the situation. Campbell's timing was perfect.

That same year the club scored a major political victory after James Budd, former governor of California, joined its board of directors and became chairman of its legislative committee. With Budd's political muscle behind it, the club finally secured passage of a "Motorist's Bill of Rights." Leaping over all local, city, and county ordinances, the new measure established a single set of uniform, state-supervised rules and regulations governing every

ABOVE: The car brought unprecedented freedom to women and men alike.

BELOW: Few places were more suited to the car than southern California. Then, as now, Santa Monica's Pier and broad beach were car magnets, c.1915.

horseless carriage in California. An idea the club had supported since its first meeting had at last become state law but the question of its enforcement remained. That question was answered when a club member—a daring individual history recalls only as "Mr. Gow"—decided to risk arrest by driving his car for several miles along the forbidden Mount Hamilton Road. Perhaps Gow was aware, as he putt-putted across that short stretch of embattled ground, that in so doing he was clearing endless miles of red tape from the paths of future motorists. The Santa Clara Board of Supervisors bent to the will of the state and let him walk away from his rebellious ride. Thanks to the efforts of the club, every highway in the Golden State was now legally open for automotive business.

The second major step came when the club helped to prepare and publish the first road map of Oakland and San Francisco. On that day in 1905, the club inaugurated a tradition of cartographic excellence that stretches to the present. Plans were also afoot in 1905 to establish a program of public service that would later become one of the auto club's most important contributions to the

THE SPIRIT OF THE ROAD

state: the posting of directional highway signs. The San Bruno Road was the first one earmarked for updating into the era of four-wheeled traffic, but several key events would prevent the signs from going up just yet.

The first came the morning of April 18, 1906, when the earth began to tremble beneath the fabric tires of the vehicles parked along Market Street. Much of San Francisco burned to the ground in the hours that followed, including the minutes of the club's April 2, 1906, meeting. The fire also bumped up the cost of widening the road along Ocean Beach to the Cliff House—a project to which the club had already donated $2,500. Perhaps the members of the club sensed amidst the rubble of the disaster an unforeseen stroke of good fortune: with an entire city in need of rebuilding from scratch, opportunities for progress abounded.

Meanwhile, it was becoming evident that the Automobile Club of California was in need of reorganization. While the club claimed to represent the motorists of California, its membership and political sway were still largely confined to San Francisco. If the motoring torch were to be carried forward any real distance, the club would have to expand its membership—and its reach. By the end of 1906 other auto clubs cropped up in San Jose, Fresno,

LEFT: Looking east on San Francisco's Market Street shortly after the 1906 earthquake.

1900-1912: THE VEHICLE OF PROGRESS

19

1905

● *U.S. auto production reaches 25,000—up from 2,500 in 1899.*

1906

● *On April 18 a massive earthquake and fire destroys much of San Francisco, killing an estimated 2,500 people and leaving 250,000 homeless. The ACC regroups within a month to continue its mission.*

1907

● *U.S. auto production rises to forty-three thousand.*

● *The first long-distance motorcar rally begins in June, involving five cars which make their way from Beijing to Paris. The winner arrives in France on August 10th.*

● *Leaders of the Automobile Club of California form the California State Automobile Association, bringing together local auto clubs from all over northern and central California. Leon P. Lowe, President of the ACC, becomes CSAA's first president.*

● *CSAA affiliates with AAA.*

1908

● *The Model T Ford is introduced. This four-cylinder, 20 horsepower car gets close to 25 miles per hour on a good road. Buyers have their choice of colors—as long as they want black. Cost is $850.50 per car.*

● *U.S. auto production reaches 63,500 with as many as 24 different manufacturers producing cars.*

● *Half of all Americans live on farms or in towns of less than 2,500. Most horsepower on farms still comes from horses.*

1909

● *CSAA produces its first highway map of California and Nevada.*

● *U.S. automobile production reaches 127,731 cars.*

PRECEDING PAGES: San Francisco burned for three days after the earthquake of 1906. Fires destroyed twenty-eight thousand buildings, including most of downtown.

BELOW: It took a lot of campaigning, but California finally began to create a well-engineered web of paved roads. Napa Valley, c. 1910.

Stockton, and Sacramento. A sense of the adventure to be had behind the wheel of a gas buggy was clearly sweeping the West, but no unifying vision of what to do about it had yet emerged.

The man who saw the pattern in the puzzle was a San Francisco builder by the name of P. J. Walker. Walker realized that the proper course of action was to merge the many scattered clubs into one—a single organization whose efforts up and down the state could accomplish far more for the motoring public than any of the clubs could begin to individually. His plan was full of what automobilists of the day might still have referred to as "good, solid horse sense," and when he took it to Leon Percival Lowe, head of the club's Executive Committee, he was urged to contact the other Northern California clubs post haste.

THE SPIRIT OF THE ROAD

Many of the clubs balked at the initial offer to join a larger organization, unwilling to surrender their destinies to a board of directors based miles away in San Francisco. Walker assured them there was nothing to worry about. The new parent club's board, he promised, would be enlarged to include seats for every local club—with enough seats to ensure that a majority of seats would be based outside of San Francisco and Oakland. The double promise was too good to pass up. The smaller clubs took Walker at his word, and in August of 1907 the California State Automobile Association (CSAA) was born.

L. P. Lowe was named president of the new organization, and E. F. Cheffins, as secretary, became the first paid member of its staff. A social organization no more, this club's mission was to champion the cause of the motorist. Its core commitments were to the establishment of good roads and just legislation.

But a commitment to good roads in the California of 1907 meant something quite different from what it means today. The

ABOVE: Renstrom Garage was on San Francisco's Stanyan Street in 1910. It moved to the budding "Auto Row" of Van Ness Avenue the following year.

BELOW: L. P. Lowe extols the virtues of the Auto Club of California in the *San Francisco Call*, December 23, 1906.

ABOVE: Unpaved, yet reasonably broad and smooth roads linked some areas of rural California.

BELOW: As the automobile became more popular, bonds were formed between disparate groups interested in the cause of good roads. The Inyo Club bestowed honorary membership on L. P. Lowe most likely in a wise bit of networking.

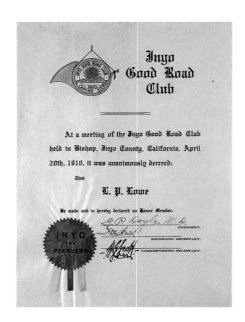

Inyo
Good Road
Club

At a meeting of the Inyo Good Road Club held in Bishop, Inyo County, California, April 20th, 1910, it was unanimously decreed:

That

L. P. Lowe

Be made and is hereby declared an Honor Member.

PRESIDENT.
RECORDING SECRETARY.
CORRESPONDING SECRETARY.

cities and towns of Northern California had been expanding unabated since the Gold Rush but the roadways connecting them still belonged largely to the wild. Something of the dauntless, trailblazing spirit that had carried men and women over the Rocky Mountains in covered wagons was required of CSAA's first members, who, sensing the link with their forebears, sometimes referred to themselves as "autoneers." Motorists who ventured outside major cities bumped along dirt roads and skirted pothole after pothole, pulling over every few miles to contend with a punctured tire or an overheated engine.

And if the roads themselves were treacherous, the vehicles sputtering along them—few of which had tops, fenders, windshields, or lights—were no better. CSAA members were expected to stop their cars and offer assistance to stranded fellow motorists, assistance that usually came in the form of a spare tire. The handing over of a spare was considered a club duty, and no sensible member set out for a Sunday drive without three or four extras.

Meanwhile, CSAA members around the state were hard at work realizing the club's first and most pressing goal: smoothing out the road ahead. Local clubs throughout California held "road-building days" in their communities, events at which members took up shovels, loaded gravel carts, and tugged split-log drags along formerly undriveable country lanes.

The club, under Lowe's capable command, was posting its first highway signs at last. It also took its first major leap outside of California—signing on as a member of the national AAA, which had been formed in Chicago in 1902. The fates seemed to be smiling on the automobilist at last. But some rural opponents of the new auto-friendly roadways were less than pleased by the new developments. Indeed, certain farmers were enraged by the sight of rich, cap-and-goggle-clad city folk tooling noisily along once-deserted back roads. Stories circulated of ranchers who quietly allowed their irrigation ditches to overflow the roads, hoping the resulting quagmire would keep Sunday drivers at home. Some of the opportunists helped swamped drivers out of mudholes by day—for a fee—and refilled the holes with water at night.

BELOW: Filling stations could be few and far between in rural areas.

MOHAWK VALLEY GARAGE BLAIRSDEN CALIF.

1910

● CSAA's president is now P. J. Walker, whose offices are in Market Street's Monadnock Building. He will head the club until 1916.

1911

● CSAA's dues are $3.00 per year.

● The U.S. has 1,000 miles of concrete road.

● Voters in the state of California grant women the right to vote.

1912

● CSAA prints its first tour book. This guide details numerous routes from Mexico to the Oregon border.

1913

● CSAA hires David E. Watkins as its first general secretary. Watkins, with a reputation as a "spark plug," will head the club for 40 years. "You knew when David Watkins was in the room," remarked an early employee. "He was a dynamic individual."

● Ford Motor Company's assembly line reduces the time it takes to build a car from 12.5 hours to 1.5 hours.

1914

● CSAA establishes its Inter-Insurance Bureau in May, and pays its first claim to Mr. C. E. Cumberson in August. Rates are 30 percent lower than established insurance companies. George Chalmers will run the bureau until 1952.

● James Johnson of CSAA's Engineering Department patents CSAA's distinctive yellow diamond road signs.

● The first red/green traffic signals appear on the streets of Cleveland.

● U.S. cattle ranchers herd cattle with Model T Fords.

● W.W.I begins in Europe.

1913–1929:

The Motorist's Champion

ABOVE: The club's race monitor car, 1922. A club-sanctioned race was, according to *Motor Land*, "No haphazard affair."

OPPOSITE: Lake Tahoe.

*I*n 1913, the momentum propelling the automobile into every corner of American life must have seemed unstoppable. Annual sales of luxury motorcars—priced between $2,500 and $7,500—had surpassed eighteen thousand, with Packard and Pierce Arrow leading the way. And Henry Ford's new $550 flivvers shut the mouths of many who had attacked the automobile as a faddish collector's item, available only to the super-rich. In October of that year, the Ford Motor Company would introduce the assembly line, an innovation that cut the production time for a single motorcar from 12.5 hours to an hour and a half. While the average American worker was still pulling in just over two dollars a day, the mass-produced dream of a Model T in every garage was drawing ever closer to reality. Meanwhile, the advent of the electric self-starter eliminated the labor of hand-cranking a car's engine to life, and its appearance encouraged

31

ABOVE: One of CSAA's many services for drivers in the 1920s was free brake testing—important in a time when most cars had only rear brakes.

BELOW: Before painted stripes were common on roads, motorists tended to drive in the middle of the street—the better to avoid such scenes, c.1917.

thousands of new drivers—many of them women—to climb behind the wheel. The newly arrived era of roadside breakdowns and blowouts even produced its first popular song: Grant Clarke and Byron Gay's, "He'll Have to Get Under—Get Out and Get Under."

Into the midst of this automotive boom stepped two men who would help to shape the fortunes of CSAA over the course of the next four decades. The first, elected in April of 1913 to the board of directors, was a slightly built, scholarly individual with penetrating eyes and an air of sober determination: San Francisco barrister Percy Towne. Towne (no relation to Burton) would go on to become association president in 1916, a post he would hold off and on for twenty-eight years. Called "the conscience of the motorist" by one CSAA historian, Percy Towne laid down in the club's formative days the bedrock sense of principled fair play that has guided its decisions ever since. The "rules of the road," as drivers understand them today owe a tremendous debt to Towne's own personal sense of justice—indeed, they can sometimes be

traced back directly to his authorial pen. When two cars approach each other on a steep mountain grade, and the driver headed downhill backs up to yield the right of way, he is heeding not only the law but also the carefully reasoned advice of Percy Towne. But if Towne was the conscience of the motoring cause, David E. Watkins—hired that October as general secretary—was its first full-time crusader. Watkins was CSAA's true commander-in-chief during its most dynamic years of expansion.

A no-nonsense Nebraska lawyer whose baby face belied his iron-willed dedication to the club and its members, Watkins provided the drive that transformed CSAA from a struggling one-man concern into a nationally recognized force in the motoring world. But when he reported for his first day of work, the club's prospects could hardly have been described as bright. After parking his brass-radiatored motorcar, Watkins strode down Market Street to the Monadnock building and rode the elevator to CSAA's tenth-floor "offices."

He found a small room leased to P. J. Walker, a room with the paperwork of the statewide organization sandwiched into one corner. At the time, the club boasted two salaried employees and claimed no more than five hundred members. Its bank account showed a balance of two thousand dollars. Forty years later, when Watkins surrendered his post as its day-to-day manager, CSAA would be serving nearly 300,000 members from forty-seven different district offices.

Watkins set up shop and got straight to work. His confidence was buoyed by a rock-solid belief that the goals he had been

ABOVE: Club officers, November 1917. Top l. to r.: L. A. Nares (1st vice-president); Percy Towne (president); J. A. Marsh (2nd vice president). Bottom, l. to r.: David Watkins (secretary); R. H. McKaig (3rd vice-president); George Forderer (treasurer).

If anyone personifies everything that is good about CSAA, it is by all accounts David E. Watkins, who ran the organization for forty years, from 1913 until he retired in 1953.

Born on a farm six miles north of Auburn, Nebraska, Watkins decided early that the farming life was not for him. Or perhaps his father decided for him. In a memo prepared on the occasion of Watkins's fortieth anniversary with CSAA Fred Hamann wrote, "Noting early that his son did not have the 'green thumb' of a farmer, nor the inclination to plow a straight furrow, his father sent him to the State Normal at Peru." Farming's loss was motoring's gain.

A CORNHUSKER MAKES GOOD

Following his Normal education, Watkins earned a law degree from the State University at Lincoln in 1904. He practiced law in South Dakota for a time, then headed west. Watkins fetched up in Los Angeles and, after one brief stint as an attorney for a cleaning and dyeing establishment, and another selling automobiles, he landed a job as a recruiter for the Automobile Club of Southern California. Watkins turned out to be brilliant at the job, and soon decided to return to Nebraska and start an auto club there. This he accomplished in short order, so he then moved on to start a club in Kansas, also with swift success.

Watkins's salesmanship and leadership soon caught the eye of CSAA president P. J. Walker who invited Watkins to become the general manager of the young and struggling organization.

It was 1913. The club had five hundred members, a staff of two, and two thousand dollars in the bank. By the

time Watkins retired, the club had grown to 281,000 members, boasted a staff of 1,300, and had opened forty-seven district offices to serve members.

Back in 1913, though, the club was struggling. But Watkins had a vision. As *Motorland* reported upon his retirement, Watkins "envisioned that the efforts of organized motorists, properly directed, could place California in the forefront of the motoring world, make it a premier tourist state, and advance the motoring welfare of the nation." Many would argue he was not only bold, but also right.

The growth of the organization and its services over the next several years was extraordinary. In rapid succession, Watkins introduced car insurance, emergency road service, the road-signing program, the auto licensing service, and *The California Motorist*, later to become *Motorland*. (All these and many other innovations are discussed at length elsewhere in this book.)

Yet despite this evident creativity and drive, Watkins was, in *Motorland*'s words, "modest and publicity-shunning." When he retired from CSAA, the board of directors presented him with a plaque "attesting to his faithful service and loyal devotion to duty" during the years he guided the organization.

ABOVE: David E. Watkins, 1926.

LEFT: Watkins offers a hearty handclasp to driver Dan Nee, who was about to drive the club Locomobile in a caravan dramatizing the need for a proposed "Park-to-Park Highway" linking eleven Western national parks, 1920.

hired to accomplish were ones any sound-minded individual would readily acknowledge. The establishment of good roads, fair automotive laws, and a comprehensive set of services for the driver—who could argue that these were not the motorist's due? What's more, Watkins believed, along with the board, that California's spectacular natural beauty and mild climate could be combined to make it the premier tourist state in the nation.

In order to accomplish this, Watkins would need the support of like-minded individuals up and down the West Coast. He turned without delay to the business of securing it, traveling south for what would be the first of many meetings with Standish Mitchell—his counterpart from the Automobile Club of Southern California (ACSC). Another member of AAA federation, the ACSC had been in existence since 1900, a year when the romance of the horseless carriage had clearly seized more than a few minds. At a strategy session that would inaugurate a close working relationship between their respective clubs—a relationship still vigorous almost ninety years later—Watkins and Mitchell agreed on priorities: a state highway system, a uniform vehicle code, and some dependable means of funding road construction. The two also agreed on another fundamental principle: each club would provide full services to the other's members.

BELOW: David Watkins wears the skimmer. Burton Towne, CSAA director from Lodi, is beneath the cap, and A. L. Westgard is suitably dressed for his job as AAA scout. Odd man out is Don Nicholson, second in command at CSAA, 1920.

1915-1919

1915
● San Francisco "Welcomes the World" to the Panama Pacific International Exposition. As part of P.P.I.E. the first transcontinental telephone call takes place between Thomas Watson, in San Francisco and Alexander Graham Bell in New York.

● C.S.A.A.'s Touring Bureau is formed to offer members maps—as well as up-to-date road conditions and travel advice for the entire state. George "Pop" Grant will head this department until 1947.

● Ford's one millionth car rolls off the production line.

1916
● C.S.A.A. creates its Good Roads Bureau to advocate for—what else?—an expanded and improved network of good roads. The department is headed by the indefatigable Ben Blow.

● A federal highway act authorizes a five-year program of aid to states for construction of post roads.

● The U.S. National Park Service is created by an act of Congress.

1917
● C.S.A.A. begins publishing The California Motorist, predecessor to Motorland magazine.

1918
● W.W.I ends.

● C.S.A.A. membership reaches 7,500.

1919
● The California Motorist becomes Motor Land.

● C.S.A.A. board creates the Forestry Department which raises $100,000 toward purchase of 20,000 acres of north state redwoods—which will become Humboldt Redwoods State Park, and later Redwood National Park.

STOP!

The DIAMOND STOP and TURN SIGNAL makes night driving safe.—   PRICE . $15.00
1657-59 VAN NESS AVE.
SAN FRANCISCO. CALIF.

"He is free from danger who, even when safe, is on his guard. —Syrus.

ABOVE: Standard equipment on new cars commonly did not include such items as bumpers, heaters, and signal lights. Diamond brand ad, *Motor Land*, May 1919.

While 1913 marked the arrival of two of CSAA's most important leaders, 1914 saw the introduction of two of its most influential services. The world had had over a decade to accommodate itself to the spectacle of a buggy tooling over the roads without a horse, but in 1914 it was still uncertain what to make of the sight of two of horseless buggies colliding head on. Insuring automobiles was a risky new venture, and rates were steep. When members called upon CSAA to do something about the situation, P. J. Walker convened a meeting with representatives from many of the major casualty insurance firms on the West Coast. Walker's argument was simple. As CSAA members belonged to a club dedicated to the principles of safe driving, a club member was better versed than the next driver in the rules of the road, and had a stronger commitment to upholding them. These factors, Walker believed, made it obvious that a club member deserved to pay less for auto insurance than the average driver. However well reasoned his arguments might have been, Walker's plea cut no ice with the insurance representatives. Walker retaliated with a threat: If the good driving records of his club's members were not recognized with some form of rate reduction, CSAA would be forced to protect their interests by starting up an insurance firm of its own. The insurers were unmoved. "Any such venture," they told him, "would go broke in six months."

Walker returned to the board determined to prove the "experts" wrong. In April, Senator John Stetson sat down with a handful of the club's other directors to figure out how to turn a threat into a functioning business. The directors voted to take advantage of a new state law, which allowed CSAA to form a not-for-profit insurance company for its members. The CSAA Inter-Insurance Bureau (CSAA I-IB) was born.

They would need someone who knew the ropes to run it, someone with enough actuarial expertise to handle the new risks posed by this newest of vehicles. They found him in the person of George Chalmers. On the first of July, the CSAA-I-IB opened for business at the club's tiny Monadnock Building offices. The bureau consisted of Chalmers himself, three staffers, and a stack of yellow-and-blue insurance forms. Amazingly, the bureau also had a twenty-five thousand dollar buffer against disaster: a personal pledge of $2,500 each from the board's directors toward payment of insurance losses. That the directors were willing to finance the fledgling bureau out of their own pockets is testimony to their remarkable faith in the association and its goals—as well as to the trust they placed in the steering and braking abilities of its members. Their pledge is all the more extraordinary since they served on the board as volunteers, none of them earning a dime for their efforts on its behalf. But the board's confidence in the venture paid off: after two years, the Inter-Insurance Bureau earned more than enough to cover its operating costs independently, and the pressure on the directors' pocketbooks was relieved. Through the years, the CSAA I-IB and its members have proved themselves more than worthy of that first show of faith. Indeed, the venture doomed to go broke in six months was writing $100,000 in premiums by 1918 and has gone on to become the largest insurer of private passenger cars in northern California.

The second service department created in 1914 may have done more than any other to simplify the task of piloting an automobile through the state of California. It was founded in response to a situation that for over a decade had had drivers flummoxed. On arriving at many major intersections, an eager motorist would find his or her forward momentum stopped short by a confusing array of hand-posted road signs. Erected by firms or individuals

ABOVE: An East Bay grocer with a top-of-the-line 1912 Oakland touring car was among CSAA's first insurance policyholders, July 1914.

OVERLEAF: San Francisco's Panama Pacific International Exposition celebrated the brand new Panama Canal and the city's rebirth following the earthquake and fire of 1906. Nineteen million people attended, 1915.

ABOVE: An unknown group rallies early drivers to form a club and affiliate with the "California [State] Automobile Association"—date unknown.

TOP RIGHT: The club pushed hard for bond issues to improve roads. The cartoon is from *The California Motorist*, November 1917.

shining sea were scarcely better than they had been for the pioneers. But the tab for a network of highways stretching from San Francisco to New York was one only the federal government could afford. In 1916 CSAA joined AAA in lobbying for the Federal Highway Road Act, which passed into law the same year. At last Congress was poised to enter the road building business, though with a world war still raging overseas, it would take a few years for the government to make good on its commitment. In recognition of AAA's support for the bill, President Woodrow Wilson presented the pen with which he had signed it to AAA.

Expansion was the order of the day, and in the years following World War I the Club's roster of services kept growing. Once roads were being properly posted and—bit by bit—paved, members needed to know how to use them to get from one place to another. In 1917, CSAA established a Touring Bureau devoted solely to the needs of the traveler, and brought in George "Pop"

Grant to run it. The department would publish a full array of maps, drawn up according to James Johnson's mile-by-mile surveys. Red lines for highways, blue for dirt roads, plus detailed accounts of elevations, grades, and mileage from point to point. CSAA representatives were also dispatched throughout the state to keep tabs on any threats to the motorist's progress. If a bridge had been washed out or a pass shut down for construction, club members could telephone for up-to-the-minute reports on the best route around it. Members were ringing up with such inquiries in record numbers: four thousand a month by 1917. How can I reach the summit of the Chowchilla Mountain Grade without boiling over? Is the rumor I heard true—that I can waterproof the top of my car with double-boiled linseed oil? And what about that awful squeaking sound my wooden wheels let out on every corner?

ABOVE: CSAA cartographers hard at work designing new maps, c.1924.

OFFICIAL
HIGHWAY MAP
of the State of
CALIFORNIA

COPYRIGHTED AND PUBLISHED BY THE
CALIFORNIA STATE AUTOMOBILE ASSOCIATION
1622-1628 VAN NESS AVENUE
SAN FRANCISCO. CALIF.

ABOVE: Official CSAA highway map, c.1915.

LEFT: 1920 map of Santa Clara.

RED—*Paved Highways and Oiled Roads*   BLUE—*Gravel or D*

ROADS OF
SANTA CLARA COUNTY
PREPARED BY
CALIFORNIA STATE AUTOMOBILE ASSOCIATION
150 VAN NESS AVENUE SAN FRANCISCO CALIF.
Scale in Miles
Copyrighted 1923

NOTICE TO MEMBERS: Should you find incorrect any information given in connection with this map, you will confer a favor, and assist in perfecting the service, by reporting same immediately to the Home Office, 150 Van Ness Avenue, San Francisco, enclosing this map.

WESTERN UNION TELEGRAM

Form 1206

CLASS OF SERVICE DESIRED	
Fast Day Message	
Day Letter	
Night Message	
Night Letter	

Patrons should mark an X opposite the class of service desired; OTHERWISE THE TELEGRAM WILL BE TRANSMITTED AS A FAST DAY MESSAGE.

Receiver's No.

Check

Time Filed

NEWCOMB CARLTON, PRESIDENT   GEORGE W. E. ATKINS, FIRST VICE-PRESIDENT

Send the following telegram, subject to the terms on back hereof, which are hereby agreed to

San Francisco, Calif.
August 28, 1918.

D. Doig,
Auto Club of Southern Calif.
1344 South Figueroa St.,
Los Angeles, Cal.

Highway Altamont to Livermore complete with exception short stretch in good condition.

Collect.   Geo. S. Grant.

RIGHT (TELEGRAM): CSAA and the Auto Club of Southern California communicated regularly in order to give members of both clubs up-to-date information on road conditions throughout the state.

RIGHT (SIGN): In 1910 ACC handled road signing duties for CSAA.

BELOW: The Touring Bureau behind its mahogany counter in the new headquarters building at 150 Van Ness in 1928. The bureau (later to become a department), the building, and the counter all are still in place.

The best way to answer their questions, Watkins and company decided, would be to put together a magazine dedicated to the modern automobilist. A first step in that direction, jointly published with a sports digest and entitled *Pacific Golf and Motor*, proved too slight to do their topic justice. News of the invention that was transforming the American landscape simply did not deserve to be tucked behind fifty pages on putters and properly fitted cleats.

Club members needed a magazine of their own. In August of 1917 CSAA gave it to them: a monthly called *The California Motorist*. Its slogan followed the club's sworn precepts: "Good Roads, Just Laws, and All Auto News." Early issues provided touring tips, dozens of maps, and advice on everything from fuel economy ("use a 50% mixture of kerosene.... Nearly all carburetors will handle this mixture without trouble") to the latest fashions.

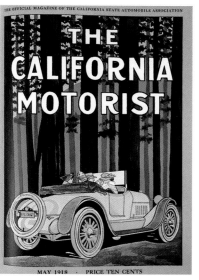

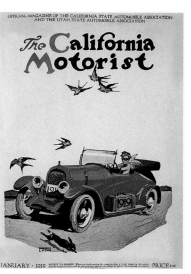

ABOVE: *The California Motorist*: The
first issue (above left) went to seven
thousand members in August 1917.
Redesigned after only six months,
the upgraded magazine hit its stride
by January 1919—just before
changing its name to *Motor Land*.
Top to bottom: April 1918, May 1918,
January 1919.

BEAUTY HINTS FOR FAIR DRIVERS

by Camille Aimee

RIGHT: A woman was at the wheel on the cover of the first five issues—they all used the same picture.

FAR RIGHT: The original spread for "Beauty Hints for Fair Drivers" from the September 1917 issue.

Danger to a woman's fair complexion is one of the chief obstacles to many a long motor trip. However, this can be avoided by simple methods. A thin coating of good cold cream is, naturally, the first thing to be done before starting. This protects the skin and prevents it from being dried out by the wind. Then select a RED veil. It does not have to be of the intense variety of red, but one of the lighter shades of this color. The red absorbs the sun's rays and prevents tanning or burning, even in the hottest kind of weather.

It is well to carry a small box of lip salve on long trips, as the wind has a tendency to dry the lips and cause chapping and small cracks which are not only disfiguring, but exceedingly annoying and painful. A judicious use of lip salve will prevent this.

The latest fad in motor coats for women this season are the trench coat, very mannish, following the military idea in every respect.

Then you have coats made of Viciena or Bolivia cloth in the rookie shade; some you find with Kolinsky collars and cuffs, while others are strictly tailored.

The hats worn by the majority of motorists are made of velvet in the rookie shade, trimmed with bands of navy blue, very striking and becoming, which are being used in place of the ugly automobile cap.

The latest handbag carried by the well-dressed woman is shaped like a rustic birdhouse, the cone-shaped lid sliding over a silk cord, which forms the handle. The lid was embroidered in brown and green in a similar technique, imitating the bark of a tree and the moss upon it. A bird was embroidered in colored silk in a false opening. These are very handy while motoring.

The knitting bags which are so much the vogue now are being made of straw-hat shapes lined with gay silks and trimmed with silk fruit or flowers, or may be lined with cretonne and trimmed with appliques of flowers cut from cretonne and embroidered onto the straw. They are useful in the automobile.

1917

LEFT (CAPTION FROM 1917): Miss Rose De Verne, dressed in the new detachable skirted motoring costume which enables a woman to make any needed repairs on her machine without being hampered in her movements. This young woman has felt it her duty to learn not only the running of the car but to go into the mechanical details of the machine. She finds no difficulty in keeping a car in excellent shape and fixing any damage that may occur out on the road. Her suit is army khaki with white kid shoes and soft white cap. The skirt buttons over the trousers. It is intended for use in cities and when stopping at Inns when out touring.

LEFT: General Tire ad from 1917.

oven, enough to bake through. When done and they are cold, dust lightly with sugar, place each apple separately in oil paper for packing.

HINTS FOR COMFORT

Add to the lunch basket a package of toothpicks. You will find them handy for helping.

CREAM CHEESE SANDWICH

Mix with one breakfast cheese a half cup of walnuts, a little paprika, salt, moisten with cream and spread between thin slices of bread well buttered.

FOR THE LUNCH BASKET
TUNNY SANDWICH

Shred the contents of one can of tunny (fish) mixed with mayonnaise dressing, placing crisp lettuce leaves between thin slices of bread, spreading the mixture upon them. They are most delicious and appetizing.

GREEN BELL PEPPER AND CHOPPED NUT SANDWICH

Put through meat grinder one cup of walnuts, one green bell pepper; mix nuts and pepper into one cup of mayonnaise, and spread on thin slices of bread. They will melt in your mouth and you will ask for more.

DATE STICKS

Beat to a cream two eggs and one cupful of powdered sugar, add one cupful of walnut meat, coarsely cut, and one cup of dates, chopped, a speck of salt, and two teaspoonfuls of baking powder, sifted with six tablespoonfuls of flour. Bake in a shallow pan in a slow oven. Bake one day before using and place in tin box to keep fresh.

FROSTED APPLES

Boil six or eight apples until skins can easily be roomed without destroying shape. Have ready some clarified butter in which to dip each one as it is pulled. Cover with powdered sugar and bake in slow

FILLING FOR SANDWICHES

Stir together two tablespoonfuls of sugar, one teaspoonful of salt, one of dry mustard, and well beaten yolks of two eggs, two tablespoonfuls of cream, piece of butter, and three-fourths of a cup of wine vinegar weakened with little water. Put on a brisk fire, stirring all the time till the consistency of custard, cool and before serving stir in one-half cup of walnuts. Be sure it is cold before spreading on the bread.

BOILED HAM SANDWICH

Grind all together twenty-five cents boiled ham, ten cents sweet pickles, and one can pimentos, mix with a little olive oil.

Membership was booming and new district offices were springing up from one end of California to the other. By 1918, CSAA's yellow diamond presided over fifteen branch offices, including outposts in Oakland, Sacramento, Stockton, Fresno, Eureka, Merced, and Yosemite. While most were small enough to be managed by a single person, their appearance on the scene was a testament to CSAA's unflagging growth during the teens—and to the ever-surging popularity of the automobile. Membership ranks had now swelled to 7,500. To keep up with

the steady stream of new applications—and to ensure that the stream remained steady—Watkins appointed Fred Dewey to found its membership department.

TOP: The Stockton district office staff poses with CSAA director Burton Towne (hand in jacket pocket), c.1920.

ABOVE: San Rafael district office, 1924

RIGHT: Vallejo district office, 1928.

THE SPIRIT OF THE ROAD

CSAA's influence spilled over the California border that year as well, when George Campbell of the Reno Power, Light and Water Company opened his office to the inquiries of AAA members. Campbell's action marked the beginning of a long and prosperous partnership with the motorists of Nevada. CSAA helped support the Nevada State Automobile Association until the Depression forced it out of business in 1933. That same year, CSAA formed its Nevada Division to provide service to AAA members in the Silver State. And when CSAA Director L. A. Nares traveled east to investigate the building of a road from San Francisco to Salt Lake City, he wound up helping people in Utah establish their own AAA club. Upon his return to the West Coast, Nares recommended to the board that the road (later named the Victory Highway, then US 40, and now Interstate 80) should indeed be built, and should run though Wendover, Utah and Winnemucca, Nevada. The Victory Highway would not become a concrete reality until 1923, but Nares's trip across the salt flats resulted in the formation of the Utah State Automobile Association—widening CSAA's affiliated sphere of service all the way to the Colorado border.

TOP: The club favored a Spanish architectural motif, both in its headquarters building and its district offices. Eureka district office, 1928.

ABOVE: In the late '20s, Oakland boasted the club's most impressive district office building.

But with the roads being what they were, how was an eager interstate driver to get to Colorado or anywhere else? By 1919, a third and final bond added forty million dollars more to California's highway construction program. The spirit of the road had captured the hearts of the Golden State's electorate, with eight out of every nine voters favoring the bond. But a motorist's journey into the Great Wide Open was still fraught with bumps, bruises, and endless backtracking frustration.

ABOVE: Clarke Cottrell and an unidentified woman with a windshield sign that refers to a drive celebrating Victory Highway improvements.

YOSEMITE'S ALL YEAR HIGHWAY

by Frank J. Taylor

Motor Land

Sentinel Peak
Yosemite Valley

JULY ~ 1926

20C THE COPY

handed down in its quaint old courthouse, standing since 1854—thence to Briceburg on the Merced River and up by gradual water-level to Yosemite Valley.

So much for the new road. It is only part of the cause for celebration and jubilee in Yosemite Valley. The other part is that seventy-five years ago the first white man stood on the brink of Yosemite Valley and gazed rapt and speechless at the magnificent artistry of nature, spread out at his feet. That white man was Lafayette H. Bunnell. He was medical officer of the Mariposa Battalion, sent from Fresno to round up the Indians who had been killing and robbing miners in the Mother Lode country below. Instead of finding the Indians, the battalion found Yosemite Valley

[I]n 1855 . . . the first tourists came to Yosemite. They traveled on horseback. One member of the party was James Hutchins, who published several articles

ABOVE: By 1926 the club had a long history of helping motorists enjoy easy access to Yosemite.

ABOVE LEFT: The July 1926 depiction of Sentinel Peak is by George Mannel.

The motorist who has been promising his family a trip to Yosemite National Park, but who has never made good on the promise because of the strenuous drive over high mountain roads, will have to turn in the old alibi for a new one by August first, anno 1926 . . ., when the new all-year road to Yosemite Valley is thrown open to the public.

This new all-year road, which has been every Western motorist's dream for lo these twenty-six years, will not be a paved highway for a couple of seasons at least, but it will be one of the finest little high-gear trips in the country. The road is eighty-five miles in length from Merced on the main State highway to Yosemite Valley in the heart of the Sierra Nevada. . . . Inside the park, a mile or two above El Portal, is a short stretch where second gear may be useful, but this section of the road is already being paved by the National Park Service. The route from Merced leads to Mormon Bar and Mariposa, historic old gold mining towns—the latter famous for the important mining claims decisions

ABOVE: Eagle Peak, more commonly known as the Three Brothers, punctuates the skyline on the north rim of the canyon.

BELOW RIGHT: Cadillac dealer and broadcaster Don Lee was a major *Motor Land* advertiser for many years. His San Francisco dealership has been restored as a theater.

and a book that further advertised Yosemite. In 1864, Hutchins settled in Yosemite and built the first permanent structure in the valley. That same year, 1864, Congress paused long enough in its worries over the Civil War to set aside Yosemite Valley as a national reservation under the State of California.

This act, creating Yosemite National Park, was so hastily passed that its provisions led to some curious developments in later years. The act turned Yosemite Valley and the Mariposa Grove of Big Trees, thirty miles apart, over to state officers for administration, but gave them no authority over territory surrounding these areas and now in the park.

Later, in 1890, the Federal Government created a national park of the area surrounding Yosemite Valley. This was administered by the U.S. Army. Thus were there two Yosemite parks, one surrounding the other. Many were the conflicts between state and federal park officials. In 1906, after officials of both the state and federal Yosemite parks had refused to fight a serious forest fire in Illilouette Canyon, each claiming it was

the other's duty, public opinion demanded that Yosemite be made one park....

An idea of the road condition of those early days can be gleaned from the reports of the first motorists to negotiate the Wawona Road. They boiled, but they need not apologize, for they were driving a tiny Stanley Steamer, equipped with bicycle wheels and tires. F. H. and A. E. Holmes of San Jose were the intrepid brothers who staged this first "call of the open road run" to Yosemite, all by themselves. Friends tried to dissuade them, but the Holmes brothers made the run to Yosemite and back in July of 1900....

The arrival of the little auto in Yosemite was viewed with much alarm by the authorities in the park. Those were the days when small boys ran miles to see an automobile and horses ran miles to get away from them. The park officials finally solved the problem by prohibiting any more automobiles from entering Yosemite. That ban held for thirteen years. In 1913, the automobile was recognized as a mountain going means of transportation and drivers were allowed to bring their machines to the valley, where the autos were chained up until the owners were ready to leave the park. To explore Yosemite Valley, the motorist could hire a horse or walk.

This and other annoying restrictions harassed the motorist to Yosemite until 1915, when the horsedrawn stages that carried travelers from the ends of the railroads at El Portal and Raymond were replaced by motor stages. Since that year, it has been the policy of the National Park Service to help and encourage motorists en route to Yosemite in every way possible. Under this policy Yosemite has become the motorist's National Park. This can be seen most clearly from registration figures. Three out of every four visitors to Yosemite this season arrive in the valley in their own machines.

The first transcontinental railway was completed in 1869 with the celebrated driving of a golden spike at Promontory, Utah. For the next many decades rail was the principal mode of transporting both people and goods across the country. By contrast, a transcontinental journey by automobile was for a long time an adventure reminiscent of the earliest trips by covered wagon.

BLAZING A TRAIL

Following World War I, some who fought in Europe began to think that if America were ever forced to fight a war on home soil, it would be dangerously easy for an enemy to sever contact between the East and West Coasts if their connection depended on a single rail line, or even two or three. Blow up a bridge or two, and the country would be hamstrung.

In 1919, Army brass decided to investigate just how difficult it would be to take a convoy of vehicles and men from Washington, D.C., to San Francisco, a feat that had never before been attempted. They rounded up more than seventy vehicles—sixty trucks, a dozen autos, plus a handful of motorcycles with sidecars (these numbers varying a bit from report to report). Some sported modern pneumatic tires, the rest the solid-rubber variety. Both types were "cut to ribbons," according to press accounts, some pneumatic tires lasting only fifteen miles. There were about twenty-four officers and 260 enlisted men (these numbers varying too, depending on the source), and the entire trip covered

3,251 miles. The men and vehicles averaged ten to fifteen miles per hour and logged an average of less than sixty miles per day. They followed the route of the proposed Lincoln Highway, roughly the same route as is traversed by U.S. Highway 50 today.

Along the way, the soldiers built or rebuilt sixty-five bridges damaged by their crossing, hauled trucks out of ditches, and pushed and dragged the vehicles across a great sand dune in the middle of Nevada. The group left Washington, D.C., on July 7, and was greeted by large crowds all along the way. CSAA officials H. R. Basford, L. A. Nares, and D. E. Watkins greeted the convoy when it entered California and escorted it into Oakland and San Francisco. *Motor Land* reported that members posted 1,200 CSAA signs along the route with the message; "U R on Your Way 2 San Francisco Bay." They arrived on September 6, only five days behind schedule. The journey had taken a total of sixty-two days. Newspapers called the trip "Homeric."

One of the officers on the journey was a young lieutenant colonel named Dwight David Eisenhower who had fought in Europe in the Great War. He and the others were sobered by the difficulty of the journey they had under-taken. Later, as commander of Allied forces in World War II, Eisenhower was greatly impressed with the autobahns in Germany, and thought the United States should undertake to build a similar system of interstate and defense highways.

CSAA, for its part, had long favored a hard-surfaced road across the country, and the 1919 trip seemed to endorse its necessity.

Congress first saw an interstate highway system proposed in 1936, but it was not until 1952, when General Eisenhower was elected president, that the idea got the champion it needed. Ike made it one of his highest priorities. The Interstate Defense Highway System was born in 1956.

In July, a convoy of army trucks set out from Washington, D.C., to investigate the viability of long haul, coast-to-coast travel on the Lincoln Highway. Sixty-three days after it set out, the caravan slogged into San Francisco, where it was greeted by CSAA President H. R. Basford and a horn-tooting crowd of well-wishers. A sobered Col. C. W. McClure, leader of the expedition, would report: "We have gotten

ABOVE: Goodrich tire ad printed in a 1918 *California Motorist* magazine.

LEFT: This photo of a Model T sign truck appeared in the August 1923 *Motor Land* captioned: "Patrol cars of this kind repair and replace damaged signs."

through over the Lincoln Highway by pushing, shoving, and the will of God." The caravan's transcontinental odyssey made the state of America's roadways clear to onlookers from Portland, Maine, to Portland, Oregon—and ensured that improving them would be a top priority for lawmakers of the next decade.

It was also clear that California's expansive new highway system, touted as the finest in the nation, was already crumbling beneath the demands of increasing traffic. With forty million new road-building dollars at the ready, CSAA wanted to make sure that the monies from the third bond would be well-spent. They dispatched one of their new directors, a structural engineer named H. J. Brunnier, to oversee a comprehensive report on the condition of the state's highways. Brunnier's team of experts

ABOVE: CSAA and the Automobile Club of Southern California jointly funded an engineering study of the state's highways in 1921.

RIGHT: Membership cards for 1923 and 1924.

BELOW: A Shell gasoline ad from the '20s made use of California's lovely coastline.

Quick Starting SHELL gives you the best gasoline that careful refining can produce.

SHELL COMPANY OF CALIFORNIA

came back with shocking news: in many cases, the roads built by the first two bonds were structural disasters. In an attempt to stretch limited bond funds to build as many miles as possible, the state had made many roads too thin. The pressure of hundreds of thousands of automobile tires was rapidly turning the roads to rubble. What's more, some members of the state commission were dead set on finishing the job they had started, and were prepared to use the same specifications to do so. Determined to prevent the squandering of another forty-million dollars, Brunnier sprang into action in Sacramento, lobbying for thicker roads and engineering standards that would stand up to traffic. The Great California Highway Fight began. By the time of its resolution, two acrimonious years later, CSAA had succeeded in writing new engineering standards for state highways—and devised a new way to pay for them. In place of bonds, CSAA fought for and won a groundbreaking new "pay as you go" method, in which a two-cent tax on each gallon of gas sold in California would cover the cost of paving its roads. The passage of the gas tax was a major victory for CSAA, and jolted California back into the lead in the race to provide a safe, efficient road network for the United States. Careening into the twenties on what looked to be an increasingly golden course, the club watched its membership double and double again. Nineteen-eighteen's already hefty tally of 7,500 card-carrying CSAA-ers would explode to fifty thousand by 1925, and then leap again to ninty

58

thousand before the decade was out.
Californians had clearly taken a shine to
the efforts of Watkins, Towne, and the
rest. To better serve these members,
CSAA consistently added new services.

In 1920, Towne presided with
Senator John Stetson over the creation
of a legal department, which provided
members with free legal advice in the
event of auto-related wrangling. The
Public Safety Department, created in 1923, worked with local
officials and police to establish some of the nation's first School
Safety Patrols, which are still active today. Many prominent
Americans served in these patrols: President Jimmy Carter, U.S.
Senator John Warner, Olympians Bruce Jenner and Lynette
Wooderd, twenty-one astronauts including John Glenn and the
space-endurance record holder Norman E. Thagard. CSAA even
sponsored a short-lived San Francisco glass patrol, in which a
goggled motorcyclist was dispatched with broom and dustpan to
sweep up glass and other debris following car crashes.

Motor Land

JANUARY · 1921   20c. The Copy

ABOVE: The infant new
year can't have enjoyed
a comfy ride as pictured,
but the '20s proved a
golden age for the car.

BELOW: A motley crew of
CSAA-sponsored safety
patrol boys, 1920s.

1925-1929

1925

● *CSAA moves into
its landmark new head-
quarters at 150 Van Ness
Avenue in San Francisco,
the building was designed
by renowned S.F. architect
George W. Kelham.*

● *CSAA also opens
the first district office—
on Oakland's Grand
Avenue—built by the
association.*

● *A Ford roadster costs
$260. During an era of
growing labor activism,
the Ford Motor Company
initiates an eight-hour
day, five-day-a-week
workweek for its workers.*

● *CSAA membership
reaches the 50,000 member
mark, making this club the
second largest in the world
behind the Auto Club of
Southern California.*

1927

● *There are now 20 million
cars on the road in the U.S.*

● *The 15th million Model
T Ford rolls off the
assembly-line.*

● *Charles Lindbergh makes
the first successful, nonstop
transatlantic flight, going
from New York to Paris, in
just over 33 hours.*

1929

● *Emergency Road Service
bows to pressure and now
offers tire changes to able-
bodied men, as well as
women and the disabled.
This prohibition had led
to actual dishonesty among
members as countless
husbands were forced to
hide nearby as their wives
had tires changed.*

● *CSAA now has 750
employees and 30 district
offices.*

● *In June, 50,000 San
Franciscans celebrate, and
"autoists toot their horns,"
as the Great Highway and
Ocean Beach Esplanade at
the western edge of the city
are completed.*

● *The stock market crashes
in October and the Great
Depression looms.*

None of CSAA's initial fleet of tow trucks started life as a truck. Many early luxury cars offered power and size, however, and depreciation on such cars was swift. Since a used car could easily be converted to road service trim in the club's shop, big used cars bought at bargain-basement prices became the basis for the club's tow car fleet.

EARLY EMERGENCY ROAD SERVICE (ERS) EQUIPMENT

A pair of Alcos, bought to equip seasonal tow-car camps the club opened near Yosemite, formed CSAA's first tow car fleet in 1922. The approximately ten-year-old vehicles originally were luxury cars built by the American Locomotive Company. Alco's six-cylinder cars, which the company said were America's most expensive, cost from $6,000 to $7,250 in 1912. With its 134-inch wheelbase and 579-cubic-inch engine, an Alco was a formidable machine. Although the Alcos were described by one early ERS man as clumsy and difficult to drive, the club soon added a third.

With the introduction of regular ERS in April 1924, the fleet expanded. The club bought a couple of 1914 Packards and at least one Locomobile of approximately 1920 vintage. These, too, were customized in the company shop.

Many early tow cars did not have a crane. Since most passenger cars at that time had a solid front axle, a dolly could be slipped under the axle, and the car raised using leverage supplied by the dolly's long bar. The tow had to be at very low speed, but there were few cars on the road so hefty that towing them could make an Alco or Locomobile tow car breathe hard.

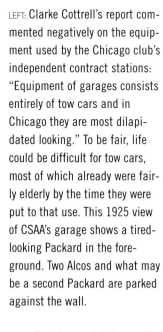

LEFT: Clarke Cottrell's report commented negatively on the equipment used by the Chicago club's independent contract stations: "Equipment of garages consists entirely of tow cars and in Chicago they are most dilapidated looking." To be fair, life could be difficult for tow cars, most of which already were fairly elderly by the time they were put to that use. This 1925 view of CSAA's garage shows a tired-looking Packard in the foreground. Two Alcos and what may be a second Packard are parked against the wall.

RIGHT: This Locomobile began life as a hard-top touring car. The 1926 photo shows it ready to accompany a motor caravan from San Francisco to Salt Lake City commemorating efforts to improve that section of the Victory Highway. Unlike the vehicle and the event, the people are unidentified.

BELOW: Although Clarke Cottrell found Harley-Davidson the best motorcycle to use as a service vehicle, after a few years, the Harleys were phased out and replaced by light trucks.

Then, as now, many ERS calls did not require actual towing. A car might need a jump-start, a spare tire installed, or some water poured into the radiator. Light-duty service vehicles were used for such calls.

Before offering ERS, CSAA sent Clarke Cottrell, its good roads expert, to visit clubs that already had the service to analyze how they did it. Cottrell reported motorcycles were the way to go for service vehicles and that they should be Harleys. "The motorcycles of the Chicago club are all Harley-Davidsons," he wrote. "The Chicago club claims this is by far the best make and they selected this type of equipment after very unfortunate experience with lighter machines." CSAA spent six hundred dollars each on eight sidecar-equipped Harleys.

OVERLEAF: CSAA's ERS fleet, spring 1924. This photograph appeared in *Motor Land* magazine in April 1924 and shows most of the club's initial fleet. An Alco heads the lineup, and the tip of a towing dolly appears over the roofs of the first three cars.

ABOVE: An unidentified, but obviously well-traveled couple parked their Maxwell in front of the club's 1628 Van Ness Avenue headquarters in 1925.

OPPOSITE TOP: A sporty couple enjoys the California good life, including the open road. Did it get any better than this? *Motor Land*, October 1923.

OPPOSITE: The club's headquarters, 150 Van Ness Avenue, under construction in 1925. Dudley Perkins is still in the neighborhood, and the school district building (tower at left) still stands.

While all these departments have distinguished themselves through the years, none has meant more to members than Emergency Road Service, established in 1924. Founded as a summer service for motorists bound for Yosemite, where club trucks rescued cars that boiled over, suffered punctured tires, or otherwise came to grief, ERS would spread its safety net statewide before the end of the year.

With club activities expanding in so many directions, it became apparent CSAA needed a new and larger home. In April of 1924, it purchased its first piece of real estate on the corner of Van Ness Avenue and Hayes Street in San Francisco. Expansion had driven the club out of the Monadnock Building more than a decade before, but its second headquarters at 1628 Van Ness were now proving equally cramped. Architect George Kelham was brought in to draw up the art deco-flavored designs of what

THE SPIRIT OF THE ROAD

would become CSAA's permanent address—150 Van Ness Avenue. The completed building (seven floors plus a mezzanine) opened its doors for business in late 1925. The association it housed was an unquestionable success. As it approached its fourth decade of existence, CSAA could boast thirty-one district offices, a muscular list of road-building victories, a host of unequaled motoring services, and a membership closing in on 100,000. Its once derided enthusiasm for the horseless carriage must have seemed at the time like an endless ticket to ride on the road to prosperity. But every road has its blowouts.

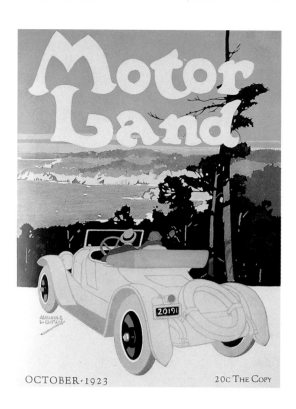

OCTOBER·1923   20¢ THE COPY

Weathering the Storm

ABOVE: A '37 Chevrolet at Washington's Tunnel Tree.

OPPOSITE: The Golden Gate Bridge.

merica's boom years went bust on October 24, 1929. The selling frenzy that engulfed Wall Street sent the Dow tumbling 30.57 points (from its perch at 380) and by the end of the year it had lost nearly half its value. The crash effectively broke the back of the nation's economy; the Dow would continue to plummet, bottoming out at sixty in 1932. In October 1929, twenty-billion dollars vanished nearly overnight—a sum almost equal to what World War I cost America's taxpayers.

The Great Depression spelled the end of CSAA's long streak of sky's-the-limit expansion. Running on three decades of momentum, the association's membership would continue to

HOW TO SPOIL A VACATION—PROPERLY:

SOME OF THE BEST WAYS ARE MADE PLAIN AS MR. AND MRS. TALK THINGS OVER

by Earle Ennis

One of the best ways to spoil a vacation is to take a wife along!

"Who said that?" demanded Carol.

We were planning our vacation in the customary manner of long married folks. That is, I was making suggestions and she was discarding them like a cook getting rid of strawberry hulls.

"Oh, Patrick Henry or Ingabord Crane, I've forgotten which."

"Just let me ask you something," said Carol with ominous quiet. "Who left the can opener home last year?"

"Oh, that . . ."

"Who forgot to change the oil and burned out a bearing?"

"Well, as to that . . ."

"Who hung the bacon over an ant's nest? Who forgot to get ice? Who thought eggs could be carried on the running board? Who prodded the wasp's nest? I'm waiting!"

When a woman says she is waiting—and waits, it is time to shift quickly, either to the right or left or to Siam. . . .

"There's one thing," I said, "I'm not going to bring along any more tight shoes

ABOVE & RIGHT: The July 1934 *Motor Land* included a characteristic mixture of travel and safety information.

to wear in a hot climate. For first class vacation spoilers, give me tight shoes."

"And I hope you won't get on a horse, like you did last year, and ride 30 miles the first day and then have to hire two men to pull your feet together so you could sit down when you got home." said Carol. "You moaned for three days—straight."

"Well, who lay on a beach on her stomach until she was so sunburned she had to go to bed for two days, all greased up like a railroad curve? I'm waiting!" I thought I'd try a little of that myself. But Carol only sniffed.

"I didn't lie down on my back in a patch of poison oak and break out in three million blisters," she remarked. "You turned your vacation into a field day for ointments. . . ."

"And with all we took, we took too much," I replied. "This time we are going to travel light. You kept saying 'Take this and take that' and presently the old bus was loaded down like a highway truck."

"And not too well loaded at that," replied Her Highness. "I recall we kept dropping things all along the road. I remember trucks, and motorcycle cops, and strange motorists driving up and saying: 'Is this yours?' That spoiled the vacation for me. You never loaded a car right in your life and you wouldn't listen to me." Another sniff.

I decided to take a firm stand. you simply cannot shilly-shally with a woman. . . .

"Look here," I said. "If this is the prospect ahead for the year why go on a vacation? Why not stay home and do the wrong things and be miserable in some sort of comfort?"

"Why not take a vacation, do the right things and quit spoiling it?" she asked.

That sounded like a sensible idea.

"How?" I asked.

A devilish light came into her eyes.

"Take your wife along and listen to her suggestions," she said, softly. Trapped, b'gee! Caught by the hind foot. I returned to the Association road map.

"All right—where are we going this year?"

Carol gave me a winning smile.

"You pick the place, darling, and I'll pick the equipment for the trip and it will all work out without the slightest friction in the world, and we won't spoil the vacation."

"Fine," I said. "That simplifies everything. Now let's see—we'll get out early, make a fast run to Los Angeles and take in the beaches, the movie studios and drop

down to San Diego and across into Mexico. It will be great down there this year. I've always wanted to loaf around the south for a couple of weeks."

Carol smiled and nodded thoughtfully. . .

The telephone rang. Carol answered. A woman friend . . . They talked about this and that. Presently . . .

"Oh, we were just talking about it. You know, running over placed we'd like to go. I rather think we are going to drive up to Yosemite this year, rest a while, take in some of the High Sierra trips and save a few days for the trip over to Tahoe. Oh, yes, but we'll take in Southern California some other year, yes . . ."

How not to ruin a vacation? Don't ask me. It has to be learned like tax evasion or alimony dodging. If you can keep your wife from wearing hiking pants; if you can remember your Association membership so you'll have tire changing service and not try to switch a rubber doughnut on a wheel at 90 degrees temperature; if you can stay single or become a temporary bachelor; if you can do these things with a smile while your sunburn aches and your gnat bites smart—you will enjoy your vacation.

And take along the sunburn lotion. There is nothing that prevents a vacation being spoiled like good, cooling sun-burn lotion.

"I'll get the lotion," said Carol.

"I thought I was to buy that," I said. "You picked the place to go didn't you?" She wrung her hands.

"Must we start all over again?"

I guess we'll have to. That's the only way to spoil a vacation—properly.

ABOVE: Any vacation at all was beyond the reach of many in the middle of the Depression. This ad is from the July 1934 *Motor Land*.

THE BABY TAKES TO THE ROAD:
TIPS FOR MOTOR TRIP TAKERS WITH CHILDREN

by Diane MacDonald

ABOVE: This June 1938 cover featured a photo poetically captioned "Wooded slopes meet placid waters at Blue Lakes, in Lake County."

If there's a baby in your family and a car in your garage, there's no reason why the two shouldn't get together this summer. Trip taking is one of the biggest joys in our modern lives and thanks to the simplified aids to baby care and the "anticipated emergencies" gleaned from experienced trip-takers-with-children, traveling needn't be foregone even by the fondest parents....

Youngsters are naturally restless and shouldn't be expected to put up with long nonstop rides. Occasional stops for swims, sightseeing and romps on cool, shady lawns will work wonders with their dispositions.

The restless age (and there's really no age limit to this rule) should be taught to respect the door handles in your car. "Hands off" should be an iron rule and it's up to you to see they're safely locked before you start out. Too, youngsters should never be allowed to stand up in either the front or back—a safety measure too often overlooked.

To keep children comfortable and entertained while you're driving, make sure there's no top-heavy luggage which may fall against them. Don't expect them to keep happy wedged in between a case of breakable bottles and a fragile layer cake. Pack your car so there's plenty of room for them, they'll need it! And a "game place" can easily be arranged on the floor between the front and back seats in case the scenery fails to entertain them. Taking games along for the children is just as much a part of congenial traveling as is "playing" games with signs along the road, license plates, etc.

Tiny infants can most comfortably travel in a basket with their regular bedding plus an extra blanket or two and an extra soft padding for "bump protection." Also, a large piece of mosquito netting will protect them from flying insects which may find your car an interesting place.

And speaking of insects, it's entirely unnecessary to have pandemonium prevail. When a bee buzzes his way inside the car, the simplest way to prevent hysteria and needless excitement is for the driver of the car to pull off the road immediately, stop, let the children get clear out of the car if they want, and proceed to eliminate the bumbler!

But back to our tiny babies . . . for short trips the swinging canvas beds in

ABOVE & RIGHT: Child safety
seats are an old idea, 1938.

which a baby can stretch full length are used by some. But still better and a wise investment, because it serves at home as well as on the road, is a specially designed affair called a "carrying baskenette." It has folding legs so arranged that one pair can remain lowered in contact with the car floor while the other end of the baby's traveling bed (with legs folded) is supported by the car seat. This makes for comfort, security, and convenience.

And for bigger babies the auto seat is a grand invention. There is a new one on the market with steel runners which fit down behind the car seat cushion and with straps for the child's shoulders and waistline. No danger of falling or being

thrown into the windshield; hence, safety for the child and peace of mind for the grownups.

If your child is at the "sit up" age place him so he can see out. Also let him stretch out on the back seat several times a day to rest his bones and take a nap. . . .

The thermos is a handy way in which to carry vegetable soup or cereal cooked "without" milk for older babies. And, for new supplies, most any grocery you will encounter will carry the canned vegetables, tomato juice and canned milk so convenient to trip-taking. An occasional graham cracker, a bit of fruit or some cold milk from the thermos can break the monotony of travel for the older youngster, but don't let him get in the habit of wanting to eat constantly while en route. Set a time for the "treat" and stick to it. Then he'll have something to look forward to. The same psychology can be applied if you

know there's a swim coming up at the next town. Anticipation will keep him happy for hours, but keep your promise.

If there's more than one child in your family try rotating their seating arrangement to promote harmony. Taking turns by the window often eliminates tussles, and being allowed to "sit in front" and watch the mileage can make little boys even "sugar and spicy."

Finally, watch your own driving for the children's sake. Avoid needless, jerky stops and starts and speedy rounding of curves that might encourage car sickness—and ten to one your children will stand the trip far better than you!

In the 1930s, the country undertook public works on a grand scale, in large part to hoist itself out of the depths of the Great Depression. As part of this effort—and because there was great demand—California decided in the early thirties that San Francisco Bay needed not one, but two bridges across its waters: one to join Marin County to San Francisco, the other to connect San Francisco to Oakland via Yerba Buena Island (also known as Goat Island). Construction costs (thirty-five million dollars for the Golden Gate, seventy-two million dollars for the Bay Bridge) would be paid off through the charging of tolls.

BUILDING BRIDGES

One can easily understand the desire for bridges: a motorist in San Francisco yearning to take his chariot out for a spin was limited to heading south or boarding a ferry to the East Bay, a beautiful but exceedingly slow undertaking. The auto club had been pushing for the bridges for most of its existence, and the progress in bridge construction was followed closely and regularly in the pages of *Motor Land*. Once the bridges were nearing completion, the club, as one of its principal activities in those days, undertook to post signs on the bridges themselves and on their approaches—five hundred for the Bay Bridge, three hundred for the Golden Gate. The Bay Bridge opened for traffic in late 1936. The Golden Gate flung open its tollbooths in mid 1937.

What makes the feat of this construction all the more remarkable is that these were, at the time, the two greatest bridges in the world, by far. The Bay Bridge was the longest suspension bridge, more than eight miles, though not entirely over water. The Golden Gate Bridge was the second longest and, gushed D. R. Lane in 1937 just before the span opened to the public, the "longest, tallest, single-span suspension bridge the world has ever known."

When the Bay Bridge opened, Edward F. O'Day could hardly contain himself: "Was not the first rainbow the first bridge? Surely that arc of beauty and promise spanning the heavens high above the waters must have stirred the first man who saw it to bold engineering dreams. Deeply implanted within all of us is the impulse to overleap obstacles. . . . A beautiful bridge is one of the noblest works of man, the consummation of art happily married to science. It is blessed by near the spot once occupied by Rincon Hill.

ABOVE: Piece by piece the giant jigsaw puzzle was fit together.

BELOW: CSAA helped put the finishing touches on the Golden Gate Bridge just before it opened for traffic in 1937.

OPPOSITE: The S.F.-Oakland Bay Bridge reached San Francisco

PRECEDING PAGES: Even without finished cables, the West Bay crossings' twin suspension spans were a beautiful sight as their catwalks, gallows, frames, storm cables, and topmost gud-errichs were lighted at nightfall.

the poetry of clouds.... It is most beautiful, perhaps, when light makes magic of its nocturne darkness and still waters lovingly kiss its feet.... Yes, a bridge is a marriage, incredible fact! The bridge marriage of San Francisco and Oakland."

Not to be outdone, J. Lawrence Toole wrote six months later:"The Golden Gate Bridge! An incomparable engineering achievement flung across the mile-wide ocean inlet to San Francisco Bay! For five years San Francisco and California, and the world that passed by watched and marveled as the great bridge grew across the Golden Gate. The Golden Gate!" He then burst into verse:

> Its glittering bars are the breakers high,
> Its hinges are hills of granite,

Its bolts are the winds, its arch the sky,
Its corner-stone the planet.

The opening of the Golden Gate Bridge was greeted with four days and nights of festivity. Toole reported, "The mightiest assembly of American warships ever gathered in peace time will anchor in San Francisco Bay." From a grandstand with a capacity of twenty-five thousand people built especially for the occasion, spectators listened to speeches and music and watched three thousand costumed players perform.

The bridge tolls, incidentally, were supposed to vanish once the bills were paid, but instead have steadily increased—to pay for maintenance, subsidize rapid transit, and most recently, finance a long-delayed seismic upgrade of the eastern section of the Bay Bridge, which was damaged by the Loma Prieta earthquake in 1989.

55-MILE SPEED LIMIT ANALYZED:
EMPHASIS REMAINS UPON THE LAW'S BASIC RULE OF SAFETY

What does California's new speed limit of 55 miles per hour on the open highway really mean, and what marked effects, if any, are likely to result from this increase of ten miles per hour in the maximum prima facie speed limit?

The new State speed limit goes into effect on Saturday, September 13, replacing the 45-mile limit which has been the measure of maximum open highway speeds in California for the past ten years.

Let us try to answer questions as to the meaning and probable effects of the new speed limit by imagining a discussion by a group consisting of a member of the State Legislature, an average motorist, a traffic officer, and traffic court judge:

LEGISLATOR: The Legislature simply legalized what has become the common practice in California as to open highway speed under favorable conditions. The old 45-mile limit had become outmoded and unnecessary, by reason of the great improvement of highways and the vastly increased safety of operation built into modern automobiles. The question before the Legislature was not one of permitting more speed on highways but of providing motorists and enforcement officers with a more workable means of measuring permissible maximum speeds in the light of modern traffic conditions and their relation to safe driving....

AVERAGE MOTORIST: A speed limit of 55 miles may make me feel easier in my mind, but it should not cause me to drive any faster than I have before. As the Legislator has said, for a considerable time traffic on main highways has been moving faster than the old 45-mile limit, except at times of unusual congestion. Speeds of 50 to 55 miles are now what you usually find on the open highway when conditions are favorable. The new speed limit recognizes that fact, but I do not

Companions of the road and truest of sportsmen, ready to start on a hunting trip.
—H. Armstrong Roberts Photo.

In This Issue:
55-Mile Speed Limit Analyzed   SEPTEMBER 1941

LEFT: Page 7 of the September 1941 *Motor Land* noted, "The two chaps on the cover of this issue typify the eager anticipation of all good gun dogs who revel in a day outdoors." There was no word of the birds' state of mind.

regard it as an invitation to drive any faster than I have been doing. Like most average motorists I prefer to drive at a speed which, under prevailing conditions, will not tax my nerves or threaten danger to myself or others....

TRAFFIC OFFICER: The basic speed law is something which we, motorists and enforcement officers alike, must recognize as being far more important than the 55-mile limit, or any of the other designated speed limits. It means, for example, that the law recognizes there are times when a speed of 55 miles can be considered safe, and times when it is not safe, even on the same stretch of highway, due to the varying conditions of traffic, weather and other influences affecting safety. Let us have the judge give us a more exact definition of the basic speed law.

TRAFFIC JUDGE: As stated in the California Vehicle Code, the basic speed law declares that "no person shall drive a vehicle upon a highway at a speed greater than is reasonable and prudent, having due regard for the traffic on, and the surface and width of, the highway, and in no event at a speed which endangers the safety of persons or property...."

Putting it another way, if you are exceeding a speed limit a traffic officer is expected to use his judgment as to whether or not you are also violating the basic rule. If he chooses to give you a ticket, and you wish to make a defense, you have the right to present evidence that your speed actually was not unsafe in view of existing conditions. But the burden of proof is on the motorist in such cases, and there are many conditions, such as density of traffic, weather, proximity of cross-roads, and other factors, which the arresting officer may cite in support of his action.

LEGISLATOR: As I see it, taking the basic speed law and the prima facie rule together, these speed limits are not fixed or arbitrary but simply a means of indicating speeds which must not be exceeded unless conditions permit it to be done in safety. The new 55-mile limit is a more workable and reasonable prima facie speed limit for the open highway than was the old 45-mile limit.

There are a number of states with higher speed limits than the new California maximum. Those state include fifteen which do not have any "miles per hour" limits at all. They rely entirely upon a basic rule of safety, such as the one state in California's speed law.

Every state, without exception, has the basic speed law as a foundation for all speed regulations. It is noteworthy that states with high speed limits, or no limits, have traffic accident records which in general are as good, and in some cases better, than those of lower speed limit states. This showing is attributed to a law enforcement policy which recognizes that speed alone is not a measure of safe driving and that safe speeds cannot be defined in terms of miles per hour.

LEFT: This ad for Golden Shell oil likens its product to the imaginary cross between a rhinoceros and and ibex.

ABOVE: World War II's "Keep it under 40" campaign was designed to conserve gas and rubber.

The United States entered the Second World War at the end of 1941. This presented a dual challenge to CSAA: support the war effort, and yet minimize the effects of war deprivation on members and their ability to drive.

WAR AND RUBBER

From a distance of sixty years, one may be excused for assuming that the critical shortage to the war effort posed by drivers of private automobiles was gasoline. Gas was rationed, after all, and people were limited in the number of miles they were allowed to drive each month. The truth of the matter, was that Japan had conquered Singapore, the Malay Peninsula, and the Dutch East Indies, the source of ninety percent of the United States' crude rubber supply. Gas was rationed in order to conserve rubber, which posed particular problems to the CSAA and its members.

This situation and more were elaborated in a *Motorland* article by CSAA president Dr. Guido E. Caglieri in 1942:

Besides the direct personal benefits your membership brings to you, there are indirect benefits and a high degree of satisfaction which are derived from the part your club is playing in the general war effort. At the request of military authorities quantities of club maps have been supplied to the armed forces for use in this area. Your club's engineering department is working in cooperation with army authorities, and signposting crews are installing special signs in and near military posts and also signs to designate the various closed areas. Your club's public safety department is assisting in traffic safety in army camps, and is conducting classes in automobile mechanics and safe driving for numerous Red Cross Motor Corps and other women's units. . . . Your Club is sharing leadership in the campaign for a voluntary 40-mile [per hour] speed limit. Thus, your club emblem is a mark of patriotic effort as well as a sign of service, protection, and savings.

Dr. Caglieri went on to quote Thomas P. Henry from an open letter to all AAA club members:

Already, we have done many things and there are still many things for us to do. We have urged upon the Government the importance of maintaining automobile services. Already, we have been assured that rubber for tow trucks will be available so that you may continue to have emergency road service, which you are going to need more than ever before. We have urged that a high priority be given to automobile parts and accessories, and such priority has already been granted.

Above all, we have urged that every governmental resource, consistent with war needs, be devoted to securing tires for passenger cars to carry them over the critical period ahead. There is now under way a program of rubber production which will in time make us self-sufficing in this commodity.

Securing substitutions for materials of which there are critical shortages, maintaining fair prices to motorists and, in an over-all way, securing the recognition due the automobile as a powerful factor not only in our daily lives, but in the war effort—that is our wartime job."

CSAA teamed up with the Auto Club of Southern California to meet the challenge. Their first campaign exhorted drivers to burn less rubber by easing up on the gas. "Keep it Under 40—Drive for Victory!" read the placards members posted on the windshields of their cars. A ride-swapping campaign encouraged workers in military factories to trade lifts to and from the plant, and in so doing cut down the number of cars on the highway. A cartoon from *Motorland* in August of 1943 depicts an inventor sitting in a basket held aloft by a team of flapping pigeons—and explaining to a doubtful investor how his new rubber-less vehicle will win the war inside of a few months.

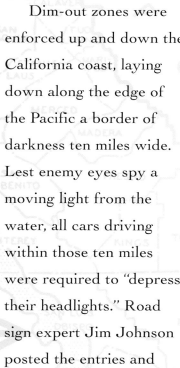

LEFT The war temporarily changed the definition of "women's work."

Dim-out zones were enforced up and down the California coast, laying down along the edge of the Pacific a border of darkness ten miles wide. Lest enemy eyes spy a moving light from the water, all cars driving within those ten miles were required to "depress their headlights." Road sign expert Jim Johnson posted the entries and exits to the dim-out zones, and put up signs explaining how and where to turn when driving in the dark. As he had in World War I, Johnson would also lead a contingent of CSAA signers overseas to post highways in Allied territory.

With so many men off fighting for Uncle Sam, the job of keeping the nation up and running fell to women in record numbers. The association sponsored free classes at Mills College and elsewhere to train women in a battery of wartime skills it thought every

1940

● *France, Belgium, the Netherlands, Luxembourg, Denmark, Norway and Romania fall to the German army. The draft begins in the U.S. in October.*

● *CSAA's Clarke Cottrell dies at age 57 and the influential Arthur Breed is elected to the board.*

● *Motor Land magazine reports that, in certain circumstances, passing another car on the right is legal, and that wearing "stylish" white gloves is the best way for other cars to see one's hand signals.*

● *Los Angeles' first freeway, the Arroyo Seco Parkway, is completed.*

● *75 percent of all drivers in the U.S. are men. This figure will change significantly in the next few years.*

1941

● *The U.S. enters W.W.II as the Japanese Navy bombs Pearl Harbor (Dec. 7th) and Germany declares war on the U.S. (Dec. 11th)*

● *U.S. auto production reaches 3.3 million.*

1942

● *The last U.S. automobile produced until 1945 rolls off the Ford assemblyline and tire and gas rationing begins.*

● *CSAA produces road signs for local military bases and establishes a Wartime Motoring Information Bureau.*

● *Horse-drawn milk delivery wagons reappear in some American cities.*

1944

● *D-Day (June 6), 176,000 allied troops land on the beaches of France.*

● *A Federal Highway Act establishes a new U.S. National System of Interstate Highways consisting of 40,000 miles of new roadways for cities with populations above 50,000.*

WOMEN WORKERS KEEP 'EM ROLLING:
THEY MAINTAIN MOTOR TRANSPORT AND AMERICA ON WHEELS

WOMEN
WORKERS
KEEP 'EM
ROLLING

*They Maintain Motor Transport
And America on Wheels*

Atop the tractor on the farm, women help relieve
labor shortage.—Lambert photo.

WHEN victory has been won and peace is restored to the world, the American woman will figure prominently on the honor rolls of World War II for the important work she now performs in wartime jobs. Honors will go to her particularly for having materially aided in the transportation phase of the war program and with having speeded the wheels that roll onward to the day of victory.

With little or no advance preparation for the arduous tasks at hand, she has demonstrated aptitude in diverse types of automotive, motor transport and motor service work for which, a few years ago, she would have been considered physically and temperamentally unfitted. But, within less than two years, the American woman has taken over these "man-size" jobs in connection with automobiles, trucks, tractors, buses, and other wheeled vehicles and is today generally credited with performing them efficiently.

Considerable of the wartime tasks so taken over was heavy, manual work customarily performed by men. Almost overnight Women War Workers made their appearance clad in the uniforms of the armed services or in the rough work clothes of the factory, shop or war plant. And one of the first jobs she tackled, and one of particular interest to the motorist, was motor transportation and its allied activities.

Today, the American woman is at the wheel of all types of vehicles or is in the service station, garage, parts factory or repair shop. In the shipyard or airplane plant, she aids in speeding production for the fighting men at the battle fronts. In the automotive and transport field she helps accomplish the homefront goal to "Keep 'em Rolling" for the duration.

It is to this end that the "service lady" measures out rationed gasoline; checks tires, oil, radiator and battery; gives the car a lubrication job, when needed, and advises the car owner on matters of maintenance. In these and all other duties she is taking over for "Joe" who is "somewhere in Italy, Alaska or the South Seas" and she performs those duties well, according to her employers.

The "service lady" does not happen to be self-sufficient and efficient by mere chance. Large oil companies, operating their own service stations, make careful selection of these women from the standpoint of natural aptitude, a ready smile and good nature

SEPTEMBER, 1943   PROTECT YOUR TIRES—5

ABOVE & RIGHT: In September 1943, *Motorland* featured an article on women's contributions to the war effort.

When victory has been won and peace is restored to the world, the American woman will figure prominently on the honor rolls of World War II for the important work she now performs in wartime jobs. Honors will go to her particularly for having materially aided in the transportation phrase of the war program and with having speeded the wheels that roll onward to the day of victory.

With little or no advance preparation for the arduous tasks at hand, she has demonstrated aptitude in diverse types of automotive, motor transport and motor service work for which, a few years ago, she would have been considered physically and temperamentally unfitted. But, within less than two years, the American woman has taken over these "man-size" jobs in connection with automobiles, trucks, tractors, buses, and other wheeled vehicles and is today generally credited with performing them efficiently.

Considerable of the wartime tasks so taken over was heavy, manual work customarily performed by men. Almost overnight Women War Workers made their appearance clad in the uniforms of the armed services or in the rough work clothes of the factory, shop or war plant. And one of the first jobs she tackled, and one of particular interest to the motorist, was motor transportation and its allied activities.

Today, the American woman is at the wheel of all types of vehicles or is in the service station, garage, parts factory or repair shop. In the shipyard or airplane plant, she aids in speeding production for the fighting men at the battle fronts. In the automotive and transport field she helps accomplish the homefront goal to "Keep 'em Rolling" for the duration.

It is to this end that the "service lady" measures out rationed gasoline; checks tires, oil, radiator and battery; gives the car a lubrication job, when needed, and advises the car owner on matters of maintenance. In these and all other duties she is taking over for "Joe" who is "somewhere in Italy, Alaska or the South Seas" and she performs those duties well, according to her employers.

The "service lady" does not happen to be self-sufficient and efficient by mere chance. Large oil companies, operating their own service stations, make careful selection of these women from the stand-

Motorland

WOMEN WORKERS KEEP 'EM ROLLING   SEPTEMBER 1943
They Maintain Motor Transport and America on Wheels

point of natural aptitude, a ready smile and good nature and health. Having passed the preliminary tests, she is then not only given thorough instruction in "pump island" duties, but is schooled in the care of batteries, tires, and car maintenance....

Nor does woman's job in motor transportation end there for she is literally "in the driver's seat" in passenger buses, trucks, taxis, farm tractors, and other motor vehicles....

Surveys made by bus and transit companies show that women employed in this field are completely "at home" at the wheel of a bus, the control lever of a street car or collecting and making change. They are credited with being courteous, obedient to orders, conscientious about their work, diplomatic in handling passengers and customers and cautious as drivers or operators.

Similarly engaged in "Keeping 'em Rolling" are the many thousands of California women taxi drivers. Hiring of "Cabettes" was instituted to meet the manpower emergency in the for-hire

transportation business. By September, 1942, some 120,000 women were employed throughout the country and the number has been steadily growing as more men enter the armed services....

Much of the light delivery work done by motorcycle is now performed by girls who also drive many of the lighter panel type delivery trucks. They are taking the place of the young fellows who delivered for the department stores, food supply houses and other retail establishments.

On the farm, too, women are taking over the task of men. They are in the driver's seat atop the tractor, keeping the fields ploughed and farrowed, and essential foodstuffs growing and going to the fighting and home fronts.

Counterparts of these women engaged in general civilian motor transportation are the many thousands of women who, in the uniform of the armed forces, the American Red Cross and the American Women's Voluntary Services are similarly furthering the war effort in transport services....

Also high in the lists of women workers who are directly contributing to the winning of the war, is the driver corps for the American Women's Voluntary Services. The AWVS woman, although required to pass First Aid examinations and basic military training, is chiefly concerned with motor transport service....

In addition to this vital role to "Keep 'em Rolling" in motor transportation, women war workers are likewise engaged in the equally important task of keeping "America on Wheels" for the railroads and street car systems where they have, after passing rigorous tests, earned from men

ABOVE: In a reversal of the usual procedure, the club (on behalf of the military) collected maps from its members.

LEFT: The original caption for this photo identified the woman as a "Moore Dry Dock motorcycle attendant."

workers the enviable title of "Angels of the Right of Way...."

When the history of war transportation on the Pacific Coast is written, some of the most glorious chapters will be devoted to the western women who left the comfort of their homes to take those grimy jobs so essential to keeping "America on Wheels."

Motorland

In This Issue: **A YEAR OF WARTIME SERVICE** FEBRUARY 1943
President's Report Reviews Association Activities in 1942

ABOVE: *Motorland* repeats its sign montage theme, this time with a wartime twist.

RIGHT: Car preservation was a major club theme. *Motorland*, May 1943.

OPPOSITE: Few scenes symbolized prosperity as well as a vast parking lot full of cars.

BELOW: Dr. Seuss contributes to the war effort, *Motorland*, 1944.

defense-minded American civilian ought to know. Participants were taught how to repair a failing engine, drive during a blackout, and circumnavigate a road bombed out of use.

Perhaps CSAA's most influential contribution during the conflict was its Wartime Information Bureau, founded to keep members up-to-date on gas restrictions, dim-out policies, and other developments a wartime driver needed to know about. The bureau sifted through an ever-growing mountain of memos, statutes, edicts, and recommendations handed down from the government, plucking out anything to do with automobiles. It kept club members informed both through its grapevine of district offices—where staffers answered questions in person—and the pages of Motorland each month. When Allied soldiers stormed Omaha Beach on June 6, 1944, an ending to almost six years of international combat was finally in sight. After the following year's armistice, the devastated countries of Europe began slowly to reckon up and repair the damages of World War II, while homecoming G.I.s took stock of their own gains and losses. The close of the war marked the end of a brutal chapter in twentieth-century history, and set the stage for revolutionary cultural change around the world. With the conclusion of its conflicts, America would enter a period of unprecedented prosperity, and motorists would take to the road like never before.

Motorland

35 M.P.H.

IN THIS ISSUE: MAY, 1943
HOW TO WORRY *Successfully*
ABOUT YOUR AUTOMOBILE
AND KEEP IT HEALTHY ON A RATIONED DIET

"YOU KNOW, DEAR....SOMETIMES I WISH WE'D GONE EASY ON OUR TIRES <u>BACK IN 1942!</u>"

Dr. Seuss

The Open Road

ABOVE: Although traffic jams predate the car, they had been a mostly urban phenomenon.

OPPOSITE: The Big Sur coast.

*I*n the wake of the armistice, America's primary task was no longer winning the war but recovering from it. As the smoke cleared overseas and the nations of Europe began sifting the rubble beneath it, American leaders were posed with a two-fronted challenge, to simultaneously lend a hand to their allies overseas while rebuilding personal and economic lives back home.

Though no shots were fired in the states, World War II took its toll on America's roads. Maintenance had been deferred for obvious reasons. Trucks hauling armaments and soldiers pounded the nation's highways for more than five years, and returning G.I.s drove home

95

across an obstacle course of ruts and potholes. In California, many roadways required a complete overhaul. With victory secure and all eyes turned to the future, the time had come for CSAA to reassess many things—including the question of how to respond to demands for new services and safer roads.

In exorcising the ghosts of the war, American motorists embarked on an extended, coast-to-coast travel spree that would last well into the fifties, and did so on roads that had not been designed to accommodate an entire nation's worth of automobiles. In 1945, the Bay Area's new twin bridges were already jammed end to end with cars—and frequently with drivers still recovering from gas rationing. In September of that year, an average of fourteen cars a day ran out of gas while in transit across the Bay Bridge. The golden age of motoring was giving way to the age of traffic congestion, but the CSAA board spotted the problem and took the lead in combating it. Among their recommendations were enlarging the toll plazas, stepping up the number of bridge-patrolling tow trucks, and instituting a penalty for drivers too sleepy to keep an eye on the gas gauge. But such measures really only slapped a bandage atop the deeper problem—too many cars travelling roads that were both too primitive and too badly beaten down to handle them. It was a problem the board believed could be solved only with a full-scale, top-to-bottom revision of the existing highway plan.

Before the war was over, director H. J. Brunnier—a structural engineer from Chicago who had come west to study the effects of the '06 quake and later helped engineer the Bay Bridge—and general manager Edwin S. Moore served on an investigative committee made up of civic and motoring groups in California. In 1945, after long hours of study and debate, the Major Highway Development Committee came to a conclusion as revolutionary as any in the annals of the American road. The answer to California's congestion problems, they reported, was the super highway.

OPPOSITE: Two-way radios began to speed Emergency Road Service calls in the early 1950s.

OVERLEAF: Did more and better roads make for more and better cars or was it the other way around?

1945

● *W.W.II comes to an end.*

● *U.S. automobile companies convert back to auto production. Henry Ford resigns as head of Ford Motor Co., and gas and fuel rationing end in August.*

● *Motorland magazine describes traffic problems on the Bay Bridge as "massive."*

1946

● *CSAA establishes its "All-Inclusive Worldwide Travel Bureau," offering members passage to "almost anywhere in the world." C. J. Stokes, a war veteran, is manager, and is replaced at his death a few years later by Fred Anderson, another vet, whose superior officer was C. J. Stokes.*

● *CSAA and other auto clubs initiate a "Take It Easy" safety campaign to slow down returning vets and others whose cars aren't in tip-top condition following the war.*

1947

● *Driver Education becomes part of California's high school curriculum.*

● *The State takes over road-signing responsibilities for major highways from CSAA, which has signed state highways since 1910. CSAA continues to place road signs on local streets and roads throughout its territory.*

1948

● *The first automobile air conditioner goes on the market.*

● *Motion-sick travelers everywhere breathe a sigh of relief as "Dramamine" is developed at Johns Hopkins University.*

1949

● *U.S. auto production reaches 5.1 million—catching up with where it stood in 1929.*

● *CSAA establishes its Approved Accommodations department, which rates and describes hotels (and later motels and campgrounds) for CSAA's traveling members.*

In the war's aftermath, the state department was looking for ways to help the devastated nations of Europe get back on their feet, and stimulating the tourist trade was an obvious solution. Back in 1939, when Germany invaded Poland, a fair number of Americans were forced to abandon their cars and return home. AAA rescued those cars and had them restored to their owners. The state department was mightily impressed, and it asked the organization to help aid its allies and boost tourism at the same time. In 1946 a group of select AAA clubs (CSAA among them) agreed to their government's request and entered the foreign travel business. The venture was a fruitful one. For more than fifty years, CSAA's Worldwide Travel Bureau has been helping members with all of their travel needs, near and far. Two other club innovations of the late forties cropped up in response to the postwar touring craze. With so many new drivers careening over the roads, crashes were becoming more frequent and CSAA realized preventative measures were needed. Not only did motorists require good roads beneath their wheels, they needed to be taught how to drive safely.

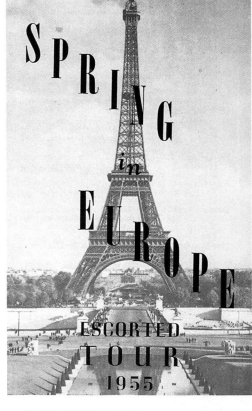

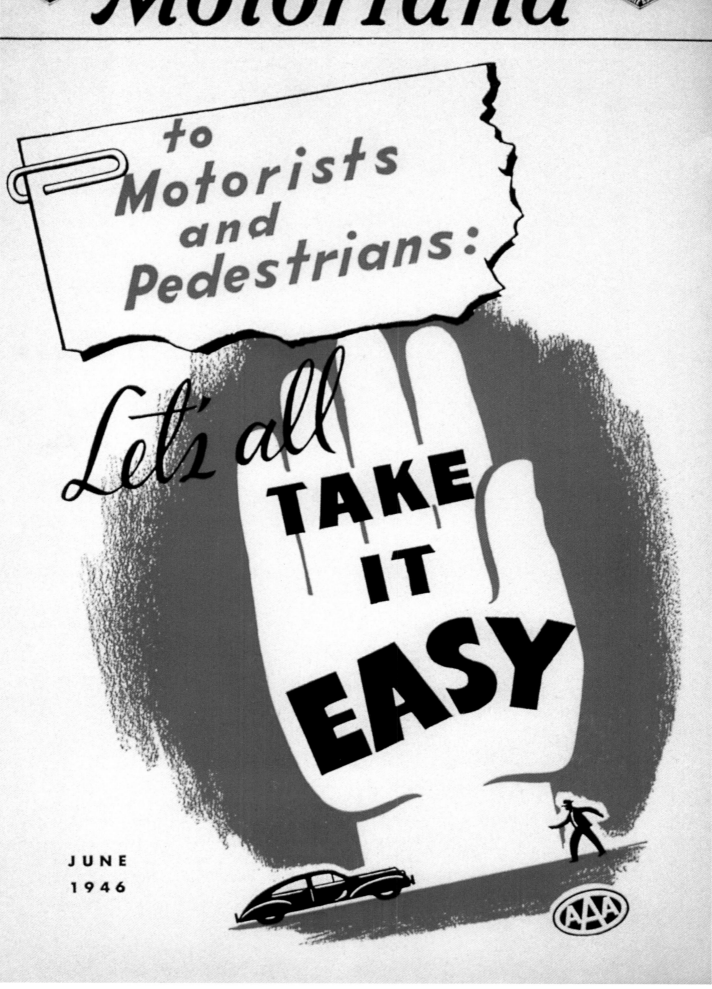

When CSAA got wind of the drivers education program Professor Amos Neyhart developed at Penn State, the board invited him out west to deliver it as a summer course at U.C. Berkeley. Neyhart's class was a hit, inspiring a grassroots movement to institute similar programs in high schools throughout the state. With CSAA sponsorship, the driver's education bill was signed into law in 1947. By 1949, every high school student in California was being taught how to operate a vehicle safely.

Families on their way to the National Begonia Festival also needed to know where to secure a good night's sleep in Capitola, Begonia Capital of the World. So in 1949, Watkins and the board came to their aid by inaugurating the club's Approved Accommodations Department. As in the twenties, when CSAA gave its stamp of approval to better garages in the Bay Area, club scouts now sought out and certified the best hotels, motels, and resort areas in the state. The sight of a yellow diamond posted in a motel's window let a road-weary traveler breathe easy, safe in the knowledge that clean beds and fair prices were to be had beneath this roof.

The touring boom of the forties and fifties was a time of staggering growth both for California and CSAA, whose membership surpassed 200,000 by 1950. In the five decades of its existence, CSAA proved its value to the state and its residents. With forty-seven district offices open for business in 1953, the club had come quite a distance from where it was when Nebraska boy Dave Watkins first reported for work at the Monadnock building.

HOW TO NEGOTIATE SAFELY THROUGH ICE AND SNOW

A Guide to

Improved Winter Driving

Distributed by
California State Automobile Association
Automobile Club of Southern California
National Ski Patrol System
Far West Ski Association

LEFT: Winter Driving
Guide, 1960s.

far western

Accommodations directory

CALIFORNIA STATE
AUTOMOBILE ASSOCIATION
AAA
APPROVED

AAA

See "About Accommodations"
in Introductory Pages

AMERICAN AUTOMOBILE ASSOCIATION

This book is published for the exclusive use of members. It is not for sale.

ABOVE: Predecessor to AAA Tour
Books, this 1952 Accommodations
Directory gave members lodging
recommendations for western
states from California to Texas.

SERVICE

PROTECTION

SAVINGS

FOR YOU

AS A MEMBER

OF THE

CALIFORNIA STATE
AUTOMOBILE ASSOCIATION

CALIFORNIA STATE AUTOMOBILE ASSOCIATION

LEFT: CSAA services
brochure. 1952.

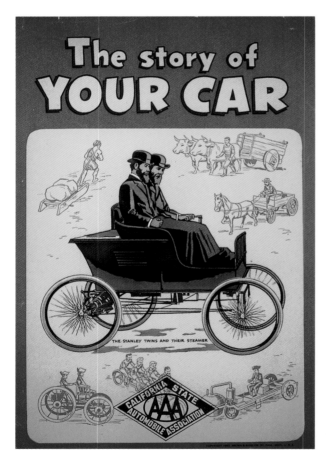

By October of that year, however, a white-haired but still bright-eyed Watkins realized the time had come to pass the motoring torch into younger hands. After forty solid years of growth, a decade-long Depression, and two world wars, the Cornhusker, as he was known to his peers, announced his retirement on October 13th.

At the same time, George Chalmers, sole head of the Inter-Insurance Bureau since its creation in 1914, made public his own plans to step down. The departure of these two leaders marked the end of an era for CSAA, but the board made sure that in losing Watkins it did not lose what he had brought to the club. A special committee chose Edwin S. Moore, Watkins's right-hand man in Sacramento, to carry on the members-first attitude that had been his boss' hallmark since 1913.

Opportunities to put that attitude into practice abounded as the association charged into the middle fifties. Moore wanted to spotlight the majesty of the Golden State in the pages of *Motorland*. The magazine had been scaled down to the size of a digest to save paper during the war, but in 1955 Moore reintroduced it in a splashy new format: extra pages, a cavalcade of four-color glossy photos, and a trim size almost as large as *Life*. The deluxe new *Motorland* premiered in March with a profile of the Sacramento Valley, and turned its attentions to a different corner of California with each succeeding month. Moore also led the modernization of CSAA's service network, improving Emergency Road Service and dramatically expanding CSAA's chain of local offices. During the '50s, CSAA also reaffirmed its commitment to preserving California's natural beauty. CSAA had worked to protect the

MOTORLAND

MARCH · APRIL 1955

The Sacramento Region

Motor Land

AUGUST · 1921   20c THE COPY

CSAA's first club publication was *The California Motorist.* The premier issue, which was pretty well received, went out to 7,000 members in August 1917. It was a lot better than what the club had been doing (using the last few pages in *Pacific Coast Golf* and *Outdoor Sports* magazine to purvey car and club information).

FROM THE *CALIFORNIA MOTORIST TO VIA*

That first issue (the magazine became *Motor Land* in 1919 and *VIA* in 1997) featured a cover drawing showing a woman in the driver's seat (and a man in the passenger seat) and proclaimed its motto: "Good Roads, Just Laws and All Auto News." It delivered, too.

Articles on road improvement vied for attention with news of pending legislation, touring suggestions, maintenance tips ("Varnish your car about every six months;" "Carbon: Autoist's Worst Enemy") and down-home information about members ("Chas. Levinson of the Union Iron Works is making a trip to Eureka;" "Elmer E. Mote is motoring to Los Angeles"). The magazine took in $12,555 in its first year, spending $15,735.

It was a decent start, but the magazine got a makeover only six months later when club exec Ben Blow, who described it as "scarcely worth patronizing," briefly took the helm.

To modern eyes, the criticism seems harsh, but an improved *California Motorist* appeared in February 1918. If not quite the "entirely new type of magazine" Blow claimed, it had become bigger and better looking. The magazine's name changed to *Motor Land* a year later when AAA members in Oregon and Utah began receiving it.

The 1920s were a golden age for cars, California, and magazines. With its great weather, rapidly growing population, and determination to build a statewide network of decent roads, California was made for the car and, apparently, for CSAA: Membership zoomed to nearly 100,000 by 1930.

In such flush times, *Motor Land* became a large, handsome publication with extensive coverage of tourist attractions and cars, poster-quality covers, and prestigious advertisers.

The magazine's enduring features appeared early: detailed travel articles, a rotogravure section with artily presented pictures of landscapes and/or cars, car maintenance advice, and advocacy—generally of better roads, protection of gas tax funds, and the apprehension of gun-toting yahoos who used road signs (many placed by the club) for target practice.

In the early 1930s, club membership sank nearly as fast as it had risen in the 1920s. Like the membership roster, *Motor Land* also shrank. Although it remained a large-format magazine, it slimmed considerably to only 16 pages. The

rotogravure section disappeared. Cover art quality declined.

Beginning with the January 1942 issue, its outside dimensions went from *Life*-like to *TV Guide*-like. Advertising and color covers disappeared. Even the name shrank, compacted to a single word, *Motorland*.

For the next few years, *Motorland* was full of war-

110

effort information for motorists: "Club Assists Rubber Collection," "Women Workers Keep 'em Rolling," "Protect Your Gas Coupons."

Echoes of victory parades had scarcely died when *Motorland* was again pushing for better roads, lauding new cars, describing driving vacations, and reminding members of club services, including the brand-new travel agency.

The small-format magazine persisted well into the 1950s, but good times were just around the corner: In 1954 newly installed club CEO Edwin Moore made plans for a bigger, fatter, full-color *Motorland*, one that expressed more fully the values of member service.

The January/February 1955 *Motorland*, last of the shrunken issues, promised members they soon would be getting "the kind of magazine you will want to keep and show to your friends with pride." The new *Motorland* arrived with a color photo of California's capitol on the cover, lots of color photos inside, and heavy emphasis on travel articles.

Motorland gradually became more consumer oriented: Travel articles strove to include all or most of the information a reader might need to take the trip being described. Articles on insurance explained, in relatively dispassionate terms, the ins and outs of coverages and recent or pending changes. An annual column outlined the most important new laws dealing with driving and insurance. Such seemingly perpetual issues as emission controls on cars, no-fault insurance, California's recurring "transportation crisis," fuel shortages, and the disappearance of lead in gasoline were regular themes. But further change was imminent.

To meet the changing need of members, CSAA's magazine needed an updated look, a new name, and a writing

style both more critical and more informative. The well-known design firm Pentagram gave the magazine's appearance a comprehensive makeover effective with the March/April 1997 issue. As part of the new design, *Motorland* became *VIA*.

In the final *Motorland*, CSAA president James Molinelli explained the meaning of the magazine's new title: "Via means 'by way of,' and we hope that in the years to come, Via will be the means by which you receive the very best information and by which you are connected to all the benefits of AAA membership."

111

GIANT TREES STAND WATCH AS THE CENTURIES ROLL ON THEIR ENDLESS WAY IN THE REDWOOD EMPIRE

Written for *Motorland* by D. R. Lane.

Northward from San Francisco, between the Pacific Ocean and the crest of the Coast Range, and extending into Oregon, is the Empire of the Redwoods. Except their cousins, the

ABOVE & RIGHT: On the cover of this May 1955 *Motorland* a Pontiac woody is photographed among the redwoods on U.S. 101 in California's Del Norte County.

"California Big Trees," which grow only on the western slopes of the Sierra Nevada, these trees are the oldest and largest of living things.

True, there are redwoods south of San Francisco, but the million acres of virgin redwood forest in the Redwood Empire are the last stronghold of

these noble trees. Scientists say that redwoods, and other Sequoias, once thrived in most of the northern hemisphere; now climactic changes limit them to the California coast.

Fossil remains indicate there were redwoods in this region millions of years ago. Many trees felled for lumber are 1,000 or more years of age and some still standing are believed to be 2,000 or more.

One reason these remarkable trees are able to attain such age is their resistance to fires which would wipe out most

forests. Even when damaged by some unusually severe burn they frequently are able to heal over the scar and go on living. There is a stump in Richardson Grove which shows the tree survived serious fires in 1147, in 1595, in 1789 and in 1806 and lived on for 113 years after an 1820 fire so weakened it that the trunk fell in a wind-

storm in 1933. This tree was a seedling about the year 700.

Redwoods 250 feet in height are commonplace. Many attain 300 feet. The monarch of them all, the Founders' Tree, the tallest known to man, is 364 feet in height. This great tree was named in memory of the founders of the Save the Redwoods League, which has done so much to conserve these great trees for future generations to enjoy....

Not age, however, nor commercial aspects, but scenic value is the factor which annually brings a million visitors to the redwoods—their towering glory, their cathedral-like calm and silence, their lush undergrowth of ferns and shrubs and their associated azaleas and rhododendrons, which in springtime make the edges of the forests blaze with glorious color.

Naturally, the road which traverses this stronghold of the forest giants is called "The Redwood Highway." Along this road you may drive for miles between trees so great they dwarf every other forest you may have seen. The celebrated "Avenue of the Giants," north of Dyerville, is a conspicuous example but there are other stretches some consider at least equal in beauty. Also along this road are most of the 65,000 acres of redwood forest in the state park system, plus many holdings in private hands.

Poets, writers, artists, photographers, have given of their best to bring something of the true feeling of these lofty forests to the public. They have all failed. It cannot be done. The only way to sense the true impact of the redwoods is to go on foot, unhurried and alone, into the depths of the lofty groves yourself.

There you may find the growth so dense that only directly above you can the sky be seen. Or near some stream, or the edge of a grove, you may see the sunlight slanting through the trees, as magical as the rays which slope through stained glass windows in some ancient church. There you may pick up a tiny cone, no larger than a man's thumbnail, and marvel that the seeds within its scales—a pound comprises 96,000 of them—could produce so vast a growth. In such a forest you may see new trees springing from the trunks of fallen monarchs, or rising in a circle from the spot where some forgotten giant grew long ago. And there, truly, you may gain a new conception of the awe and majesty of Nature....

But the Redwood Empire comprises more than forests. All along the ocean shore are bays and beaches, bold headlands and rocky outcrops where the long rollers, coasting in from their journey across the far Pacific, burst into foam and come at last to rest. In parts of this coastline, cliffs rise sheer from the sea.

This lovely shoreline, often likened to the coast of Devon, begins just north of the Golden Gate. Near Drake's Bay, the English mariner, sighting the chalk-white cliffs, was reminded of his country's coast, and so called the land "Nova Albion...."

But it is redwoods you chiefly came to see, so taking one of several roads inland, you come by a pleasant drive to the Redwood Highway and turn north. Soon the groves come so thick and fast— there are more than 40 named ones, plus many unnamed ones, in Humboldt State Redwood Park alone—that you cast aside your memories of intervening firs and other trees, you forget the streams you have crossed and the towns you have passed, and think only of the huge red-brown trunks, the dark green foliage far above and the ferns and varied other undergrowth which line the road....

ABOVE, LEFT: *Motorland* resisted the temptation to park a car in its photos of California's natural wonders more often than one might think.

BELOW: Few things get dated-looking faster than the future.

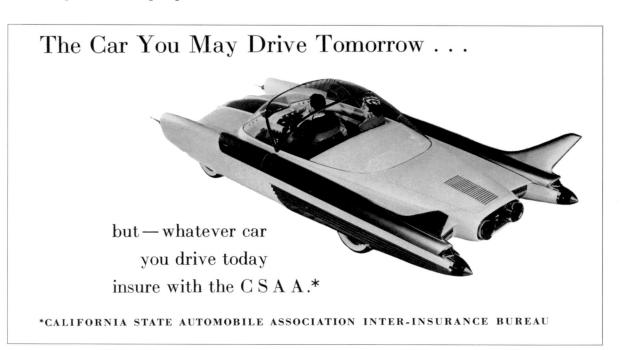

113

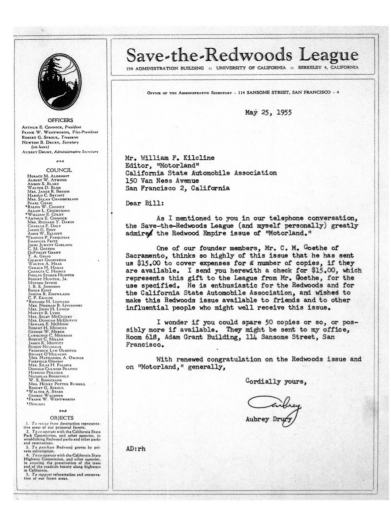

ABOVE: The second issue of the redesigned *Motorland*, devoted to the Redwood Empire, certainly pleased the Save-the-Redwoods League, May 1955.

RIGHT: The club has long supplied camping information to members.

state's natural wonders since 1919, when Burton Towne founded the club's Forestry Department. The money Towne raised in the teens sheltered some twenty thousand acres of redwoods in South Park Basin, an area that would later make up a sizable piece of Humboldt Redwoods State Park, later to be incorporated in Redwood National Park.

In 1956, CSAA helped preserve the forests of Humboldt again, this time blocking a group of developers bent on running a highway up the mid-dle of them. But all was not smooth sailing. In December of 1955, a relentless series of storms punished the northern half of the state, with floodtides as devastating as any in state history. The Inter-Insurance Bureau leapt into action, dispatching its top claims adjusters to disaster areas in Yuba City and Santa Cruz—first to help with the rescue efforts and then to assess the damage. Clad in hip-boots and waders, they plunged into the deluge alongside club members, searching for cars that had been washed off the road. Some claims were paid on the spot, as car after waterlogged car was recovered. When tallied up in terms of its damage to automobiles, the episode stands as the sin-gle most destructive in California history. For CSAA, it stands as the ultimate example of how far employees will go to assist their members.

PUBLIC CAMPGROUNDS
ON THE
NATIONAL FORESTS
IN
CALIFORNIA

U.S. DEPARTMENT OF AGRICULTURE
CALIFORNIA REGION
FOREST SERVICE
1958

DISTRIBUTED BY
TOURING BUREAU
CALIFORNIA STATE AUTOMOBILE ASSOCIATION

As the fifties rolled toward their conclusion, a spirit of transformation was in the air. California was growing. CSAA was adding new services and looking for new solutions to old problems. Traffic was challenging transportation leaders to find new methods of transporting large numbers of people from place to place. By the late fifties, a system of fixed-rail transbay trains nicknamed BART (Bay Area Rapid Transit) was in the works, but had stalled out for lack of funding. State lawmakers, unsure of the wisdom of laying an underwater tube from San Francisco to Oakland, refused to issue the necessary bonds to fund the project. Frustrated over and over in his attempts to secure a state bond issue, BART general manager John Pierce turned to CSAA for help. CSAA supported a proposal to use Bay Bridge tools to pay for bond financing of BART's transbay tunnel. This support

LEFT: Metal sign used by a CSAA ERS "Contract Station," a garage or gas station that contracts with CSAA to provide familiar yellow tow trucks in emergencies.

1955

- U.S. car sales reach a record 7.1 million. Only 52,000 of those are imports, but the appeal of cars such as the Volkswagen Beetle is growing.

- Ford introduces the Thunderbird.

- CSAA incorporates southern Nevada and Las Vegas into its territory. The Auto Club of Southern California previously counted this area as its own.

- Large scale flooding strikes northern California. Claims adjusters from CSAA aid residents in hard hit communities such as Yuba City and Santa Cruz.

1956

- The Federal Aid Highway act is passed by Congress authorizing a 42,500 mile series of interstate highways linking major cities, to be completed by 1972.

- CSAA lobbies for Redwood Highway bypass legislation, which will prevent new highway construction through the Humboldt Redwoods. The legislation is successful.

- "S.F. Discovers the Motel" shouts a headline in the San Francisco News. "Some," the article continues, "even feature swimming pools." San Francisco, which only had four motels in 1952, now has 45. The city, notes the writer, is "not as formal as she used to be."

1957

- The Soviet Union launches the world's first manmade Earth satellite. It is called Sputnik I.

1958

- London gets its first parking meters.

- CSAA membership climbs to 434,000.

1959

- Alaska and Hawaii become the 49th and 50th states.

1960-1964

1960

● John F. Kennedy is elected president.

● There is one passenger car for every three people in the U.S.

● The Datsun is introduced into the U.S.

● CSAA offers free towing to patrons of the Winter Olympics at Squaw Valley in the Sierra.

● California's State Motor Vehicle Pollution Control Board is formed. CSAA's Jack Spencer is named director.

1961

● The Soviets launch the first manned spacecraft to orbit the earth.

● Roger Maris breaks Babe Ruth's home run record of 60 in October at Yankee Stadium. The Yankees win the World Series.

1962

● California surpasses New York as the most populous state.

1963

● President John F. Kennedy is slain in Dallas, Texas, on November 22.

● CSAA purchases its first large computer, an IBM 1410.

● Two-thirds of the world's automobiles are located in the U.S. and the number of motels in the U.S. reaches one million.

● The California Scenic Highways program is created. CSAA president Edwin S. Moore is part of the advisory committee.

● The Beatles have their first big hit, "I Want to Hold Your Hand."

1964

● U.S. gas prices are just over 30 cents per gallon.

● CSAA joins the campaign for Roadside Rests (rest stops) along the interstate highway system.

● Congress passes a Wilderness Act protecting America's last remaining wild lands.

proved decisive. The bond went through. In his thank you letter to CSAA, Pierce claimed that without CSAA's imprimatur, BART never would have been built.

Expansion followed expansion, both in membership and territorial reach. In 1955, CSAA became the official AAA club for the entire state of Nevada when it opened a Las Vegas Office. In less than a decade, it saw its membership more than double, leaping from its 1950 total of 200,000 to a mind-boggling 434,000 by 1958. To cope with the volume of records, CSAA took one of its biggest steps into the future in 1963: It purchased an IBM 1410 computer. The acquisition symbolized more than CSAA's leaders could have realized at the time, for with that first computer CSAA entered the information age.

MEMBERSHIP GROWTH

1900 — 10

1915 — 3,500

1930 — 91,000

1945 — 133,000

1959 — 500,000

ABOVE: People first crossed the Bay on its surface. Later they could drive far above it. Soon they would be able to speed across deep beneath it.

ABOVE, RIGHT: Actress Kim Novak poses in the cab of a tow truck, December 1964.

LEFT: This 1960 *Motorland* chart shows CSAA membership growth between 1900-1959.

OPPOSITE: BART construction brought a ray of hope to Bay Area commuters.

THE SPIRIT OF THE ROAD

Members
First

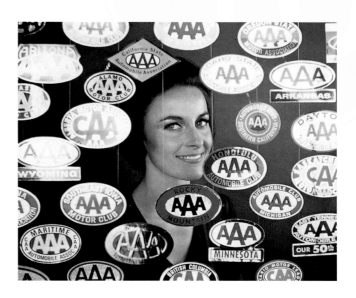

ABOVE: A woman looking out from behind a Calderesque array of logos helped illustrate the annual report for 1968.

OPPOSITE: Stormy fall sunset over Mono Lake, California.

"*M*embers first" had been a guiding principle of CSAA since Dave Watkins assumed the reins in 1913. For much of CSAA history, however, a good deal of the organization's effort was focussed on serving the public at large. Transportation policy and finance, safety programs, driver education, and licensing all had shared center stage with direct member services, such as Emergency Road Service, maps, and insurance.

As the century hit its two-thirds point, and with membership fast approaching one million (a milestone it would reach in 1969), the club realized that members wanted, and needed, help with a broader array of issues. CSAA was determined to devise new services to increase the value and improve the usefulness of membership.

Anyone who has watched "60 Minutes" or other televised versions of investigative journalism has seen examples of outrageous fraud in the car-repair business. An automobile, after all, is an exceedingly complicated piece of machinery, and its inner workings are a mystery to most. If a mechanic says your Bronson Bolt is about to fail and you had better be prepared to cough up fifty bucks for a new one, it is all too likely that you will not know that there is no such thing as a Bronson Bolt.

In the mid-sixties, CSAA began to offer free safety inspections to members—a fine service, but incomplete. Soon after, it heard about a diagnostic center run by the auto club in Holland that identified problems with autos—

RIGHT: The astronomical cost of crash parts has long made a robust contribution to the cost of auto insurance, 1966.

auto repair kit

Auto repair costs have risen rapidly in recent years. Replacing a fender on a low-priced two-door sedan now costs 25% more than in 1960. A hood costs 78% more. The average auto insurance collision claim is more than $340. That's why the most important tool in your auto repair kit should be the CSAA member's auto insurance policy. Your nearest district office has full details.

CALIFORNIA STATE AUTOMOBILE ASSOCIATION · INTER-INSURANCE BUREAU

Two automotive diagnostic clinics to serve you better

Over 100 safety and performance tests made on your car in less than an hour. Since the clinic performs no repairs, the report it issues you completely unbiased. The charge to member is $23 or $25, depending on car. An appointment is necessary. To arrange to have your car checked, call the clinic nearest you.

San Francisco, 150 Hayes Street (415) 565-215

although it did not perform repairs. This was a useful separation that promised to cut down on the incidence of fraud. The CSAA board liked the idea, and in 1968 it added this new service and opened its first diagnostic center in a building across the street from club headquarters in San Francisco.

For a nominal fee, a member could bring in a car, have it checked bumper to bumper, and get a written report of recommended repairs. The member could then shop around for a mechanic to perform the repairs—and would be well-prepared if the mechanic recommended a new Bronson Bolt. Once repairs had been completed, the member could bring the car back to the CSAA center, where

mechanics would make sure the repairs had been done properly. A second diagnostic center opened in San Mateo some years later, to be followed by another in Concord.

CSAA next tackled the issue of auto repair with a pilot project launched in 1976 called Approved Auto Repair. A shop was evaluated for quality and reliability, and if it passed, it was eligible to become an approved shop. If a member had a problem with a repair, CSAA would mediate a settlement between the shop and its member.

ABOVE: The November 1972 issue of *Motorland*.

LEFT: A CSAA patch.

1965
● *Unsafe at Any Speed*, published by Ralph Nader, expresses concerns about the over 51,000 people who die in car accidents each year.

● Congress aims to improve the appearance of U.S. highways (with the urging of First Lady "Lady Bird" Johnson) and allocates funds to remove unsightly billboards from roadways.

1966
● Neal Garrison becomes CSAA's chief executive officer. Retiring CEO Ed Moore becomes president of AAA Foundation for Traffic Safety.

● The federal Interstate Highway system is 54 percent complete.

1967
● CSAA launches its "Bring 'em back ALIVE" safety program to reduce fatal car accidents on long holiday weekends. San Francisco Giants baseball great Willie Mays is a spokesman for the campaign. In addition, free safety inspections are offered for members at CSAA contract garages.

● Use of mass transit falls dramatically in the U.S.—to eight billion people from 23 billion in 1945.

1968
● Volkswagen automobiles account for 57 percent of U.S. imports. 70 percent of these are VW Beetles, which sell for $1,800.

● CSAA opens its first Diagnostic Clinic in San Francisco, patterned after similar shops in the Netherlands. Members can have car problems diagnosed before they see their mechanics.

1969
● U.S. astronauts Neil Armstrong and Edwin Aldrin walk on the moon.

● An Automobile Accident Study Commission is created by California Governor Ronald Reagan, with CSAA's Inter-Insurance Bureau manager Richard Patton as a member.

Bring 'em back ALIVE!
CALIFORNIA STATE AUTOMOBILE ASSOCIATION

ABOVE: Willie Mays lent his celebrity to the campaign, although the slogan suggested Frank Buck might have been the person to get.

RIGHT: Sharon Kay Terrill gracefully executes one of her last official duties as Miss California as she applies a "Bring 'em back ALIVE" sticker to her car, 1969.

BELOW: This tug on the heart-strings helped illustrate *Motorland*'s "Coming Events" column in August, 1968.

In the mid-sixties, a radio staple was the dire prediction issued prior to Memorial Day, the Fourth of July, Labor Day, and other holidays that lured people into their cars for long drives. "It is predicted that 465 people will die in automobile accidents this long holiday weekend," the reports would say, and the predictions were depressingly accurate. AAA decided to do something about it, and in 1967 it launched a campaign called "Bring 'em back ALIVE," to make drivers more aware of the need to drive safely on long, getaway weekends. CSAA participated by stationing crews along busy highways and at known trouble-spots. They provided news to a large network of radio stations, reporting on traffic conditions. The club also offered advice on how to drive safely, calling attention to the information with help

THE SPIRIT OF THE ROAD

from celebrities like Tennessee Ernie Ford and baseball great Willie Mays. The campaign was deemed a success, and was continued for many years.

Soon the club branched out further, offering low-cost financing for the purchase of automobiles and, in a harbinger of intense political struggles to come, supporting a registration fee increase of $1 to support research into air pollution. In 1970, expanding on its practice of recommending good-value hotels and motels, CSAA began to give its blessing to especially attractive and well-maintained campgrounds. In 1971 the organization added homeowner's insurance to the list of products and services it offered members.

ABOVE: This illustration accompanied a *Motorland* article that promised the campaign would be extended to holidays besides Labor Day.

LEFT: *Motorland* car registration ad, March 1969.

BELOW: *Motorland* revisited a major theme of the 1930s—bridging the bay—in 1970.

Attention California motorists!
It's time to register your car for 1970.

And a convenient way to handle it — whether you have special problems or not — is through your Association's auto-registration service, available to all CSAA members.

It can be one of the easiest things you do all year . . . simply:

1. Fill out the auto-registration renewal application mailed to you by the Department of Motor Vehicles, making your check payable to the California State Automobile Association, for the amount indicated on the application.

2. Mail the application and check to the nearest CSAA office, postmarked no later than midnight, February 4, 1970.

3. A new license-plate sticker for 1970 and a validated 1970 registration stub will be mailed to you.

PLEASE don't be disappointed when you don't receive the new gold-on-blue license plates. These will be issued ONLY to new cars and cars being registered in California for the first time.

4. However, if you haven't received an application by early January, bring your 1969 registration stub to the nearest CSAA office for computation of your renewal fee. Remember, you are responsible for filing your renewal whether or not you have received an application.

5. If you have any other questions about registering—a car with out-of-state plates, an error in your application, transfer of ownership, or **any** other problem—visit a CSAA office and let our trained personnel help you.

6. Most important of all, remember that the automobile license renewal period in California is from DECEMBER 1 THROUGH FEBRUARY 4. Don't incur a penalty by forgetting to register in time.

The Mighty Bridges Span San Francisco Bay, Page 6

THE FIRST CALIFORNIANS: AS WE CELEBRATE THE BICENTENNIAL, REMEMBER THE PEOPLE WHO MET THE BOAT

by Don W. Martin

As America enters the springtime of its Bicentennial Year, California and the other states are busy with their individual celebrations.

Of course, California wasn't part of the Union when the Revolution began so most of its Bicentennial activities are concerned with the state's own roots—the Spanish padres, the gold seekers and others who settled here. But what about the original Californians?

The Indians—not the Spanish—were this area's first settlers. They established the first social order and the first communities. They were the state's first craftsmen, tradesmen and builders.

Most Indians are hardly in a mood to celebrate the Bicentennial, since the

creation of our modern society has led to the near destruction of theirs.

"No, we aren't turned on by the Bicentennial," said Modene Voeltz of the Chemehuevi tribe. "But since it's a history celebration, maybe this is a good year for the rest of California to become more aware of its Indian heritage."

Modene works with Indian Campgrounds, Inc., which has built public camping facilities on several California reservations. This is one of the many all-Indian enterprises now underway in the United States.

Many Indians have chosen to leave the reservations to join the mainstream of society as workers, teachers and artists. Others have stayed on their land to try and develop a local economy. Even as Indians merge into the greater community, they understandably want to preserve their own identities and heritage. They do this through groups such as the California Tribal Council, and with cultural festivals and Indian-operated shops. Many are bringing back the old arts, crafts and dances. The fourth Friday in September is American Indian Day in California—proclaimed by Governor Ronald Reagan in 1969—and some tribes conduct special cultural activities over that three-day weekend.

Fortunately, most of us have discarded those awful stereotype images of Indians as portrayed on TV westerns. Still, the average person probably knows little about their original culture, which was richly diversified—particularly in California.

The first Americans probably arrived in this state about 8,000 years ago (but future archeological discoveries could push that time back). They migrated southward from Canada, down the eastern side of the Sierra and entered California through the southern deserts. So southern

ABOVE & CENTER: This March/April 1976 issue of *Motorland* printed a photo of Limantour Beach at Point Reyes National Seashore on its cover, and featured an article on the first Californians.

California was likely settled first, followed by the central valleys and coasts. The north coast was probably occupied last, perhaps by later groups filtering down from the Northwest.

Through the centuries, more than a hundred tribes evolved in California, speaking dozens of separate languages. They were the Yuroc, Modoc, Hupa, Miwok, Pomo, Salinan, Chumash, Tubatulabal, Alliklik, Mohave, Yuma, Diegueno and many others. Some tribal names such as "Yahi" simply meant "the people." Other names were given to the tribes by early white settlers. Then as now, California was the most populous part of the continent. Anthropologists estimate that this area had the largest Indian population of any region in North America.

Blessed with gentle climate and plentiful food, most California tribes didn't need to develop the more advanced hunting, farming and building techniques of Indians in more hostile environments, and most were less warlike. They lived in harmony with nature—gathering acorns and other seeds, fishing and hunting. California Indians built a variety of shelters, and some constructed rather elaborate villages. In warmer climates, they often slept in the open.

This doesn't mean they were more primitive than other tribes. Their lives were quite sophisticated. Freed from the constant search for food and shelter, they developed elaborate social systems and

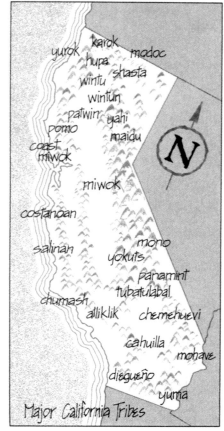

Major California Tribes

religious rituals. They played an assortment of games—even an early version of la crosse. California Indians were among the best basket-makers and sailors of all tribal groups. Obviously, they didn't just sit around a shady glen, chipping arrowheads. As one anthropologist suggested, Indians probably spent as

much time and thought making arrowheads as we do mowing our lawns.

Unfortunately, their peaceful nature was their undoing. Most offered little resistance to the European intrusion and they ultimately lost their lands to the Spanish, Mexican and later American settlers.

Few Indians actually joined the early California missions—perhaps 50,000 out of a quarter million then in the area. The padres tried to teach them new skills and work them into a European-like community, but they succeeded only in destroying their free-spirited lifestyle. The earliest explorers such as Sebastian Vizcaino had described California Indians as "affable, generous and...very merry." But after colonization, mission Indians were "sullen and dispirited," according to later writings.

Eventually, they were pushed onto reservations, usually on the state's least productive land. Isolated for years, they are now gradually being accepted as part of the California community. A few of the reservations are even welcoming visitors, for they are in rugged but beautiful areas and tourist facilities are being developed....

LEFT: CSAA was eager to help people fill the void in their driveways, 1976.

When people think of AAA, they tend to think of tow trucks, car insurance, travel tips, and maps. As is explained throughout this book, these associations are only a small part of the story, although a very important part. The very first was the creation of road maps to help members get where they wanted to go. The premier map, issued in 1909, was of northern California and Nevada.

MAPMAKER, MAPMAKER, MAKE ME A MAP

BELOW: The CSAA's up-to-date, computer-generated map of the Lake Tahoe area.

RIGHT: Map detail of Anderson, California, 1989.

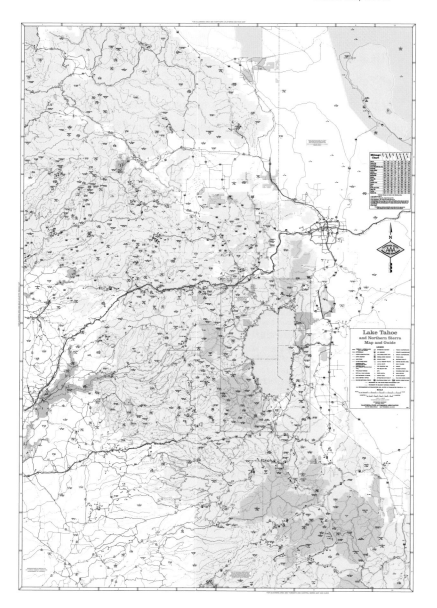

In order to make a map, the first chore is to gather information. In 1909, this involved going into the field and taking elaborate notes of the names of roads and streets, the distances between cities and towns, and a thousand other details. Early maps were hand-drawn on linen with India ink. Verbal information was set on linotypes, and printing plates were made combining the graphic with the written information.

In 1966, a new technique was introduced. "No ink is used" in the process, proclaimed the annual report, "[a]ll lines and symbols are scribed on especially coated poly-ester film by precisely ground needles and blades. All working and numbers are done by photo-typography."

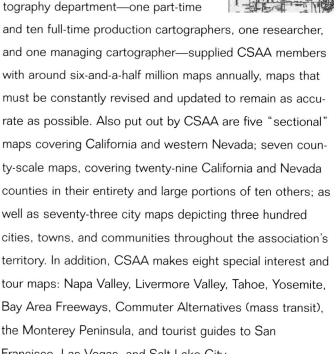

Within the past several years, as with many other arts and crafts, the computer has greatly simplified and speeded up the cartographic process, and today most CSAA maps are made with the assistance of Macintosh computers using Adobe Illustrator software.

By the end of the century, the cartography department—one part-time and ten full-time production cartographers, one researcher, and one managing cartographer—supplied CSAA members with around six-and-a-half million maps annually, maps that must be constantly revised and updated to remain as accurate as possible. Also put out by CSAA are five "sectional" maps covering California and western Nevada; seven county-scale maps, covering twenty-nine California and Nevada counties in their entirety and large portions of ten others; as well as seventy-three city maps depicting three hundred cities, towns, and communities throughout the association's territory. In addition, CSAA makes eight special interest and tour maps: Napa Valley, Livermore Valley, Tahoe, Yosemite, Bay Area Freeways, Commuter Alternatives (mass transit), the Monterey Peninsula, and tourist guides to San Francisco, Las Vegas, and Salt Lake City.

130

The gathering storm clouds finally broke in 1973 when OPEC—the Organization of Petroleum Exporting Countries— severely curtailed the amount of crude oil it was pumping from its wells and supplying to the United States and Europe.

The oil embargo hit the country hard—and nowhere harder than in California, where people depend on the automobile for most trips. Gas stations simply ran out of fuel. Lines of people waiting to buy gas stretched, sometimes, for miles, and jockeying for position occasionally turned violent. People were urged to abandon their cars in favor of trains and buses whenever possible.

CSAA encouraged members to conserve fuel, think about buying smaller cars, and use public transit. It also endorsed the national reduction of top highway speeds to fifty-five miles per hour. In a tangible innovation that would last for many years, it worked with television station KPIX, the Hibernia Bank, and the state transportation department in a carpooling venture called RIDES for Bay Area commuters.

TOP: Gas shortages in the 1970s created long lines at filling stations like this one, in 1979.

BELOW: The May 1973 issue cover story was "Easy Access to Big Trout."

Fishing, California style
Utah's red rock country
Circling British Columbia
Those add-on emission devices

Motorland throughout this period was a virtual legislative digest, carrying blow-by-blow reports of proposed and pending legislation in Sacramento, occasionally urging members to state their own views to their representatives.

CSAA continued to support proposals for improving mass transit and other fuel-saving techniques, but stuck closely to its policy that taxes on gasoline, paid by motorists, should go for construction and maintenance of highways and not be diverted for other purposes, no matter how meritorious. President Jimmy Carter had—to considerable ridicule—dubbed the challenges posed by the energy crisis and the oil embargo "the moral equivalent of war," and called on the public to conserve petroleum. CSAA endorsed conservation measures, but encouraged increased exploration for new sources at the same time.

One effect of the rising gas prices that had unforeseen consequences was the rise of the self-service gas station. As an upshot, many people neglected to check their oil, tire pressure, or coolant. This in turn caused problems that had been avoided in the past when service station attendants automatically performed those services with each fill-up. To help members avoid this trap, *Motorland* began to publish car-maintenance tips regularly.

Tensions slowly began to abate once the embargo was lifted. The association had done its part, supporting moderation in highway speeds, helping encourage and set up car pools, and urging members to consider purchasing smaller, more fuel-efficient vehicles.

Additionally, the opening of the BART tunnel under San Francisco Bay, though years behind schedule, promised to ease traffic congestion a great deal, especially on the Bay Bridge. CSAA had been a staunch supporter of BART and had campaigned hard for measures to provide financing for it.

LEFT & OPPOSITE:
Motorland featured BART in its November/December 1974 issue.

1975
● *Microsoft is founded in Seattle by nineteen-year-old Harvard drop-out Bill Gates.*

● *CSAA celebrates its Diamond Anniversary. Membership grows to 1.5 million.*

1976
● *Apple Computer is founded by two more college drop-outs: Steve Wozniak and Steve Jobs.*

● *A continuing drought plagues California: the Golden State turns temporarily brown.*

1977
● *President Carter, declaring the energy crisis to be "the moral equivalent of war," proposes a national program to conserve energy. Congress creates the U.S. Department of Energy.*

● *CSAA promotes the increasing use of child safety seats.*

● *CSAA establishes its Auto Technical Services department.*

● *California enacts perhaps the strictest air pollution laws in the nation.*

1978
● *The last of the original-style Volkswagen Beetles rolls off the assembly line in Germany, to be replaced by the Rabbit and other more '70s cars.*

● *Richard Patton replaces Neal Garrison as CEO of CSAA.*

1979
● *The Pacific Coast's Interstate 5 highway is completed. Unlike its southern cousin (the one ending in "66") it does not inspire a great popular ballad. It does, however, stretch 1,380 miles from "Ca-na-da to Mex-i-co."*

● *Chrysler, the 54-year-old automaker, is saved from bankruptcy by a loan guarantee from the U.S. government.*

● *In Las Vegas non-smoking travelers now have a friend: The Inn reserves one whole wing for those who don't puff.*

ABOVE: John Holmgren at
the KCBS microphone.

RIGHT: "Time for Travel"
notice, *Motorland*
magazine, July 1980.

Then one day, Chet Castleman of KCBS phoned to ask if someone from the association might like to turn the teletypes into radio reports for broadcast on the air. The task fell to an editor at *Motorland* named John Holmgren, who had joined CSAA in 1950 and would eventually become editor of the magazine in 1980.

Thus began the radio career of one of the most widely recognized radio voices in the Bay Area. Holmgren's reports first covered road conditions in ski season, then

became "Tips for Weekend Trips," with suggestions of jaunts to the wine country, Carmel, Big Sur, or any one of scores of possible destinations. Later the segment was called "The Road Ahead," and it ran for five minutes and aired Saturday

mornings. The spot included travel suggestions and features, like an interview on safety with the head of the Highway Patrol. Eventually the show became "Time for Travel," and aired every weekday, two minutes a pop. Often many of the commentaries were edited and compiled in book form, for distribution to CSAA members. In all, Holmgren's radio career wound up lasting thirty-four years, ending in 1994, three years after he retired as editor of *Motorland*.

Each of Holmgren's radio segments ended the same way: "This is John Holmgren of the California State Automobile Association." Neither Holmgren nor the association was paid cash for their services; instead, KCBS donated advertising time to CSAA, an arrangement that benefited the station, the association, and the public, alike.

Before there was National Public Radio, and before nearly every radio station began to air traffic reports during drive time, there was KCBS. If you lived in the Bay Area and wanted the latest news, KCBS was where you would tune your radio. KCBS, in fact, was the direct descendant of the first broadcast station in the country, which came to life in San Jose, California, on January 1, 1909.

"THIS IS JOHN HOLMGREN..."

In the '70s, in order to be able to provide its members with the most up-to-date possible information on traffic and road conditions, CSAA installed in its offices a teletype that received messages from the State Division of Highways. The association provided the information to its district offices, and also to local newspapers, radio, and television stations, which passed on bulletins to readers, listeners, and viewers.

Against the backdrop of mounting political pressures surrounding cars and highways, the Association continued to attract new members, move into new communities, and add new services. The first district office opened in Oakland in the teens and more than a dozen were added before 1920, stretching from Fresno to Eureka. The first ones were tiny, one-person affairs in rented space. But in due course CSAA began to buy buildings—or land—and erect their own buildings from scratch.

The district offices were a convenient benefit of membership, a one-stop spot where a member could register an automobile, pick up road maps and hotel guides, inquire about insurance for car and home, and get recommendations for a trustworthy mechanic. In the '70s the organization undertook a major expansion to better serve its fast-growing membership, eventually overseeing a total of seventy-six such offices throughout northern California.

Change was clearly in the air. The highway system, while it would need perpetual maintenance, was unlikely to see significant future expansion. Cars were improving steadily in fuel efficiency, reliability, and safety. CSAA was growing like Jack's beanstalk. All eyes were on the future.

ABOVE: Opening of the new Las Vegas District Office, 1978.

LEFT: Marysville district office staff, 1972.

1980–2000:
The Road Ahead

ABOVE: In Felton in the Santa Cruz mountains, CSAA assisted homeowners with questions about storm-related coverage, March 1982.

OPPOSITE: Rockefeller Grove, North Coast Redwoods, California.

*D*uring the winter of 1981–82, northern California was hammered by a series of powerful storms that caused mudslides and flooding up and down the state. Particularly hard hit were Marin and Santa Cruz Counties, where thousands of people are insured by CSAA, both for their cars and for their homes. The floods stranded thousands of cars and forced many members from their homes. CSAA sent teams into the field to seek out members in need of assistance; they retrieved automobiles washed into ditches; and they wrote checks to help homeowners cope with major damage.

Homeowners insurance policies typically do not cover earthquakes and mudslides unless a special policy is purchased. But the organization

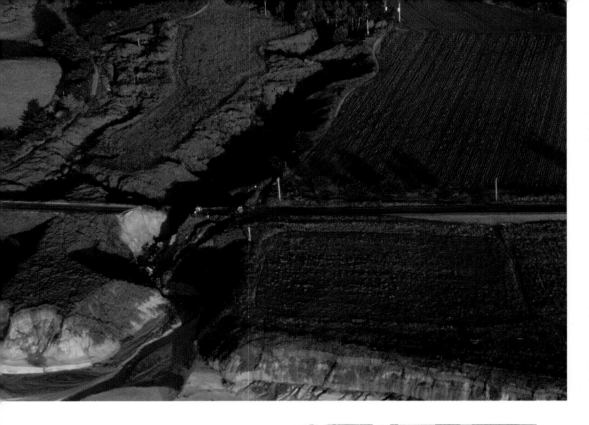

ABOVE: The storms of 1981 and 1982 caused major property damage.

ABOVE, RIGHT: Many cars, let alone homes, could not escape the ooze.

RIGHT: Claims representative Jim Lee posts a notice about coverage for storm victims in a slide area Red Cross station.

BELOW: Grateful homeowner thanks claims representative Jim Izawa in slide area.

could recognize a disaster when it saw one, and asked itself what it could do to help. People—members—were hurting. They needed help. The board of directors met and swiftly agreed to extend and expand insurance coverage beyond what was included in the standard home owner's policy. It was an extraordinary—and very likely unprecedented—decision, which prompted an interesting chain of events.

It is illegal to change the terms of an existing insurance policy while it is in force without the agreement of the insured, for obvious reasons: if it were permissible, companies could simply lower coverage once a problem was encountered. But now CSAA was proposing to expand benefits and provide coverage where none had existed before. Some CSAA competitors were clearly troubled by CSAA's decision to offer additional benefits and feared they might suffer because of it. They complained to the insurance department.

THE SPIRIT OF THE ROAD

But CSAA did not back down. It took the extraordinary step of adding benefits to existing insurance policies, benefits that provided emergency cash to stricken policyholders.

CSAA is a club after all, not a profit-making business. The well-being of members is its first concern. Then-president Brian Hill wrote proudly of this important aspect of CSAA following the Loma Prieta earthquake of October, 1989, which caused the association once again to go to extraordinary lengths to help its members. "Back in 1915, Dave Watkins ... said, 'The member comes first.' ... The member came first in 1914, when CSAA formed the Inter-Insurance Bureau to insure safe driving CSAA members on a not-for-profit basis.... Our member-first attitude enabled us to be there when our policyholders needed us on October 18." It is an attitude that has served the organization— and its members—well.

In the 1990s, CSAA began examining services offered to members to see how they might be improved and expanded. The association grew phenomenally after World War II and established district offices in all corners of its growing domain. It was now time to look ahead, to plan for the future.

BELOW: We Were There: Inter-Insurance Bureau ad following the Oakland Hills fire, *Motorland* January/February 1992.

We were there before the smoke cleared.

On Sunday, October 20, 1991, thousands of Oakland and Berkeley residents lost their homes.
But even before the fires were out, we were helping our insured homeowners, whose hundreds of claims quickly mounted into the millions of dollars.
Policyholders received cash advances, on the spot, to help with food, shelter, clothes, and transportation.

But what if you're left homeless after a disaster not covered in the policy? We can still help, with our unique "limited all peril" coverage.
Call your nearby CSAA office and ask about our Homeowners Insurance, exclusively for members. Find out about "limited all peril" coverage, the 100% replacement cost coverage guarantee, and the HELP line (Homeowners Emergency Loss Plan).

We're here to help you recover.

California State
Automobile Association
Inter-Insurance Bureau
CSAA/IIB.
A non-profit reciprocal inter-insurance exchange

1980
● *Americans suffer under double-digit inflation. Sales of American cars fall as drivers seek fuel economy in foreign models. Imports account for almost one-fourth of the U.S. auto market. Seventy-eight percent of imports come from Japan.*

1981
● *Sales of American automobiles fall to their lowest levels in twenty years. The prime interest rate rises to 21.5 percent.*

1982
● *Recession continues to plague much of the world, and unemployment in the U.S. reaches 10.8 percent— the highest level since 1940.*

● *CSAA offers members with Homeowner's Insurance limited "all perils" coverage for atypical disasters such as earthquakes and floods. Members receive up to $1,500 in living expenses and up to five percent of personal property benefits when their homes are made uninhabitable.*

● *Drivers look for the yellow diamond as CSAA initiates the Approved Auto Repair program of inspecting and rating auto repair facilities.*

● *Japanese auto sales account for 22.6% of U.S. auto sales. Honda begins building cars in Ohio.*

1983
● *In a dubious trend, Chicago motorists may now talk while they drive, as cellular phones are available for a mere $3,000 initial outlay, and $150 per month.*

● *CSAA members use Emergency Road Service 1.9 million times during this year.*

1984
● *Los Angeles hosts the summer Olympics. The Olympic Torch Relay Committee consults CSAA maps to plan its designated route and avoid losing torch bearers.*

● *CSAA's Approved Auto Repair is now available from over six hundred garages in northern California and Utah.*

GETTIN' HOLD OF BIG SUR:
HOW TO RISE ABOVE ALL THAT GEOLOGY

by Camille Cusumano

LEFT, BELOW, & OPPOSITE:
Motorland featured the wonders of the Big Sur coastline in its May/June 1992 issue.

It is the most scenic strip of tipped land on the West Coast. A huge, westward-tilting precipice, thrusting up to one thousand feet above the boiling surf.

The problem is where to get a strong hold of the jumble of bluffs, raging sea, and rising land masses called Big Sur.

There are the turnouts. The frequent alcoves cater to motorists who think that Big Sur is one big photo opportunity. At the dramatic overhangs such as Soberanes Point, Rocky Point, and Hurricane Point, you can anchor your feet on sturdy ground and safely watch the tide rip over cragged boulders, kelp forests drift toward marine terraces, the mist loll about.

But this approach has its limits. You are surrounded by a grandeur that has long aroused the eternal muse of poets, photographers, and painters. Yet a few giant steps in any direction quickly exhausts your sure footing. . . .

But you can, if you have a little stamina, take an unedited easterly hike on a fairly well-maintained trail system, penetrating the otherwise harsh contours of Big Sur.

Hiking is the way to get to the heart of Big Sur. To scramble over and around its canyons, creeks, and ridges is to appreciate its various configurations of land and water.

On these hikes you get ever-changing perspectives of the double- and triple-spined Santa Lucia range with its peaks close to six thousand feet. You can linger over the botanical riches of Los Padres National Forest and the Ventana Wilderness. You can gaze at the Pacific perhaps as well as the red hawk that circles the canyons, watching the shreds of fog from a sun-drenched vantage.

Pick up some groceries at the Fernwood or Ripple wood stores in the Big Sur Valley to fill your day pack. Carry plenty of water, bring sunscreen and, on some hikes, bug repellent. The following three hikes vary in difficulty, but all require good conditioning and some level of endurance. All three and many others are described in great detail in Hiking the Big Sur Country by Jeffrey P. Schaffer (Wilderness Press, Berkeley).

MOUNT MANUEL

This nine-mile, round-trip hike up to Mount Manuel climbs about 3,150 feet over a trail with little shade but stunning views. You can find the trailhead easily in Pfeiffer Big Sur State Park, near the baseball field. The trail's first half dozen or so steep switchbacks are often in cool fog, but within minutes you are in sun and looking clear to sea. . . .

Following, there are enough peaks and pinnacles to take your already-labored breath away. And early in the summer there'll be wild iris, Indian paintbrush, lupine, monarch butterflies, and much more. Yucca daggers, shooting up from brushy slopes, enhance the drama. At the top, amidst ponderosa pines, you have almost a 360-degree view. And it is very hot.

ANOTHER PART OF THE FOREST

The trailhead for this hike is just about two miles south of Pfeiffer State Park. You'll see a parking area on the east side of Highway 1 and a sign marking the Pine Ridge Trail.

The Pine Ridge Trail shows you even more of the diversity of ecosystems in Big Sur. You initially climb up and down over gullies and through redwoods, past riparian areas, and through mixed hard-wood stands. You spend a lot of time in the trees—first on a bench left in the ancient path of the Big Sur River. Eventually you have a view across to Mount Manuel. There'll be fewer ocean views, but a lot more shade. You'll come closer to some of the streams, falls, and springs that cut channels through Big Sur country....

KIRK CREEK TRAIL

This trail has some of the finest ocean views. They begin immediately and stay with you for a long time. The trail-head is located just across from Kirk Creek Campground on the east side of the highway (you must pay if you park at the campground.). Through a garden of paint-brush, monkeyflower, and Scotch broom you'll climb steep switchbacks, seeing white caps far out. Highway 1 swivels along below and seems to diminish to a hairline S. Suddenly there are sycamores, then a ring of cool redwoods, as the path curves east into Hare Canyon. You traverse a good deal of grassy slopes before entering the canyon. You'll see cliffs and ridges, then zig-zag up the crest of a saddle. All along your views of the coast are broad and long, running up and down as well as west. You can take this trail to Vicente Flat Camp, which is about five and a half miles out.

ABOVE RIGHT:
A November 1984
CSAA ERS
Christmas ad.

The focus of the organization at its founding had been on public service, in the form of road signs and general promotion of the automobile, driving, and highways. Later, the focus broadened to include member services, such as emergency road service, maps, and insurance. As the first century drew to a close, service to members gained renewed momentum.

In order to take a systematic look at the services members might need, CSAA analyzed the life of a person's association with his or her car. Step one is deciding to acquire a car. Step two is the purchase. Next comes getting the car registered. Then comes buying insurance. Along the way the car must be maintained. Then comes an eventual breakdown, followed by repair. Finally, one sells the vehicle and the process begins again.

CSAA has assisted members at different stages along this continuum throughout its history. First was the provision of insurance, beginning in 1914, with the creation of the Inter-Insurance Bureau. Next came assistance with registration, in 1916. A CSAA director was late for a board meeting because he had been stuck in line for two hours at the Department of Motor Vehicles waiting to register his car. He proposed CSAA seek the right to register vehicles at its district offices, and the service remains in effect today. In 1924 the Emergency Road Service (see chapter 2) came into existence to help with the breakdown part of the cycle.

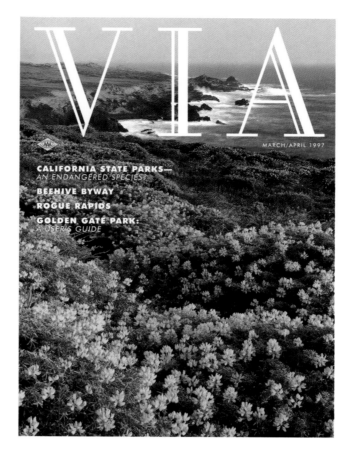

Your AAA magazine has a brand new name and a new look— *Motorland* has become VIA.

Through the 1980s, as CSAA began a long, careful examination of itself, its services, and its future, there began to be suggestions that it was time to change the name and content of its magazine. *Motorland*'s circulation was huge, more than two million copies, which put it into one in three homes in Northern California. But surveys showed that many members rarely read *Motorland*, and that potential advertisers thought it was a magazine for off-road vehicle users. "Motoring," as a synonym for driving, had passed from favor. Furthermore, CSAA was about all kinds of travel—ocean cruises, plane trips—rather than just exclusively about automobiles and highways. The idea of finding a new name was logical, but for many it was less than urgent. *Motorland* had been around forever. Why change it?

But the thought would not die and, in 1997, President

MOTORLAND BECOMES VIA

James P. Molinelli brought a proposal to the board for reinventing the magazine, enlarging the scope of its travel stories, and modernizing its photography and graphic design.

But what to call it? Hundreds of possible names were suggested and considered, only to be discarded. The best names seemed to have been taken already. It needed to be simple, easy to remember, and suggestive of the idea of travel.

Finally, associate editor Maria Streshinsky proposed the name *VIA*. It was short, memorable, and had a sly double meaning: "Road" (in Latin), and "by way of," as in "via air mail." Rendered in capital letters, it made a pleasing, symmetrical parallelogram.

There only remained the matter of a new design to go with the new name. Lynn Ferrin, editor at the time, telephoned her friend Kit Hinrichs at the distinguished graphic-design firm, Pentagram, in San Francisco. Hinrichs, who had been a CSAA member for years, said "I've been waiting for this call forever. I'd love to redesign the magazine."

And so *VIA*, a smart, handsome, modern magazine came to be in 1997. It immediately won a graphic-design award and was featured in a full-page article on the front page of the business section of the Sunday *San Francisco Examiner*. Advertising revenue, a remarkably reliable gauge of a publication's appeal, began to rise. Members reacted positively, too, spending more time with the magazine and placing a higher value on it. *VIA* is filled with evocative travel articles accompanied by the best possible color photography, the better to serve the wants and needs of its readers, who do love to travel. All in all, a worthy successor to *Motorland* and its predecessor, *The California Motorist*.

TRAINING KIDS:

GAMES, VIEWS AND GREAT ADVENTURE ON THE CALIFORNIA ZEPHYR

by Don Patton

Friends said we were crazy. The opinion was near unanimous, but it was wrong. We weren't crazy. Not yet.

From the outside, to a non-parent, transcontinental train travel with three young children might signal madness arrived or madness to come. Parents, though, soon learn the importance of marketing, of putting a good face on grim circumstances....

But in this case, we did have a choice of sorts: two-and-a-half hours by air or thirty-plus hours by rail, San Francisco to Denver.

RIGHT & BELOW: *Motorland*'s November/December 1993 issue featured a first-hand account of what it is like to travel by train with small children.

A mid-winter trip to the Rockies with our children (Sarah, age 8; Michael, age 6; and Laura, age 4) to slide in the snow, visit relatives, price real estate.

On one side of the equation: speed, convenience, high fares, and some minor schlepping of baggage from carousel to curb. On the other: the great wide West out our window; mountains, deserts, valleys, time zones, rivers, and wildlife. Retracing the history of westward migration, sharing quiet moments in the Dome Car, pointing out eagles, elk, ducks, and beaver to my son, gazing into my daughter's sweet face as she drops off to sleep, lulled by the rocking of the train, the clack of the track as we rocket through a Nevada desert shimmering under a wintry moon.

I am not making this up. Reality cannot touch the way I see things....

We started simple: food, of course, and games. Books. Crayons, markers, pencils and paper products on which to use them. Then, we got warmed up. As the insidious parent torture test—a small voice repeating "Are we there yet?"—began to echo and re-echo in our heads, our stockpile grew: puzzles, playing cards, "surprises," personal stereos, even a laptop computer. I'll do my story on it, I lied to myself, keep my notes on it. Reader Rabbit saw action between Oakland and Denver; the word processor never got booted.

That two-point pop in Nabisco stock in early January? That was us. Wheat Thins, Ritz Bits, Teddy Grahams, Nillas. (In our experience, full mouths ask no questions.) Small cartons capable of spraying juice the width of a train car when punctured by a small hand wielding a straw at six thousand feet. Enough food items to create a crumb carpet four inches deep, though I'll have to deny this until the statute runs out on the carpet cleaning bill....

Thus, departure day found us, innocents aboard, hoping for the best but geared up for a long haul....

My view of train travel is a slow-paced idyll of sweeping vistas, reflective moments, relaxed discourse fueled by the shared experience of travel. The kid's version is an action thriller: exciting corridors to explore, strangers and windows, a snack bar where Mom and Dad actually say yes to potato chips, mysterious doors that open with a whoosh to reveal a rocking netherworld between cars....

During the day, as the Sierra Nevada, the Utah desert, the Rockies offered up their considerable charms outside our windows, we played Go Fish, War, Crazy Eights and gin rummy. We dispensed goodies from the treat bag at an unprecedented rate. We supervised turns on the two personal stereos and helped Michael master Reader Rabbit. We read stories, exclaimed over hundreds of crayon sketches and works in progress and kept an eye out for animals. Michael, Laura, and I spent a happy hour in the Skyliner

Lounge car, discussing prairie dogs, snakes and clouds....

Upon our return, our friends asked, "Did you have fun?"

Fun is not the first word I would choose to describe transcontinental train travel with small children. Challenging, yes. Memorable, certainly. Fun, though, let me check my thesaurus on that.

Yet I spoke earlier of magic.

Children have a way of dispensing it all on their own. If we let them, they will shatter our old worlds and offer us a glimpse of brave new ones.

As we rolled down from Moffat Tunnel toward Denver, after a full two days of training, our trip was winding down. The night lights were on in our room; the bright lights of Denver glimmered just ahead. On one side, Michael lay asleep, bundled in his new parka. On the other, Sarah and her mother spoke quietly.

I took my soon-to-be four-year-old daughter, Laura, into my lap.

"Well, Laura," I asked, not knowing at all what I might hear in response, "what was your favorite part of the train?"

Laura squirmed around to face me. She put her hand on my arm and looked me in the eye.

"You, Daddy," she said. "Playing with you."

Crazy.

ABOVE: A CSAA ad for its Mature Driver program was printed in *Motorland*'s November/December 1993 issue.

LEFT: Drawing by Sarah Patton, age 8.

1990

● C.S.A.A. welcomes 150,000 new members in 1990— a new record!

● C.S.A.A. wins a "Silver Telly" award for its anti-Driving Under the Influence public service announcement.

● The Saturn car is introduced by General Motors to challenge Japan's hold on one-third of the U.S. auto market.

● Yosemite National Park turns 100.

1991

● A brush fire destroys nearly 3,000 homes and kills 25 people in the space of one Sunday in the Oakland hills. C.S.A.A. will pay more than $100 million to policyholders—more than twice that paid out following the Loma Prieta earthquake two years before. This fire will rank as the most destructive urban fire in U.S. history.

● C.S.A.A. will annually answer more calls for emergency road service than the California Highway Patrol.

1992

● Bill Clinton is elected president.

● C.S.A.A. introduces cell phones with a "direct to A.A.A." Emergency Road Service button.

1993

● C.S.A.A. is a proud participant in the **Hand to Hand Food and Gift Festival**, a fundraiser for **Project Open Hand** which brings warm meals to thousands of AIDS patients throughout the Bay Area.

● C.S.A.A. inaugurates its Vehicle Pricing Service.

● **Motorland** reports that nationally deaths due to traffic accidents are at an all-time low—1.8 per 100 million vehicles, due mainly to increased use of seat belts and drunk-driver campaigns and laws.

T I M E

for a check-up.

Want to save time and money down the road? Over 80 careful checks can show where repairs or replacements are needed. Includes unbiased written report and free Car Care booklet. Smog inspection and specialized checks also available. Just call for an appointment.

Your CSAA Auto Diagnostic Clinics:

Concord (over 80 tests $40) . . . . (415) 671-2708
Reno (over 80 tests $40) . . . . (702) 826-8800
Sacramento (over 80 tests $40) . . . . (916) 331-7610
San Francisco (over 100 tests $45) . . . . (415) 565-2155
Santa Clara (over 100 tests $45) . . . . (408) 247-5405
Santa Rosa (over 80 tests $40) . . . . (707) 544-1010

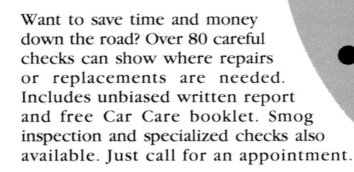

ABOVE: Auto diagnosis was a big step toward the club's aim of helping members in all aspects of car ownership.

A diagnostic services program to help in the maintenance phase came into being in 1969, and the Approved Auto Repair program in the '70s and Car Care Plus in the '90s were designed to assist with repairs.

CSAA also undertook a similar effort with respect to insurance itself. First, it sells a policy. Next, it collects the premiums. Then, when a crash occurs, it writes a check to cover damage or losses. To help reduce the number of crashes, CSAA has instituted dozens of safety programs—through teen-education programs, Otto the Auto, anti-drunk-driving campaigns, and many others. It has also taken steps to speed along the process of filing and collecting on claims.

THE SPIRIT OF THE ROAD

You might think teaching traffic safety to five-year-olds was the height of futility, but you'd be wrong. It is never too late, it is said, but it is never too early, either.

A case in point is Otto the Auto, who began visiting kindergarten through second-grade classes in California, Nevada, and Utah in 1991.

AN AUTO NAMED OTTO

Otto teaches kids to look all ways before they cross the street, always buckle their safety belts, and other lessons designed to permit them to live long lives.

Otto is a robot, controlled by a Wizard-of-Oz-like person who hides behind a curtain. (Please don't tell the kids.) Otto can move forward and back, spin in a circle, wink his headlights, and talk. Live talk, not taped. Kids ask questions, Otto answers.

Marcella Escobar, who spent several years hauling Otto to schools in and around the Bay Area, says the effect is quite extraordinary. Having an adult lecture such young kids about safety simply wouldn't work—they'd fidget, start pinching each other. But when this little car—it is about the same size as they are—cruises into the classroom and begins talking to them, they are riveted. Questions come in a torrent. The most common? Where does he sleep? (In a garage.) What does he eat? (Gas and oil.)

As of late 1999 there were five Ottos throughout the CSAA service area, each one costing around $6,500. Each Otto visits many schools and safety fairs each month, meaning that something like 200,000 kids hear Otto's good advice every year. The children really fall for Otto; many write him letters. So recently, Otto got his own Web site (www.ottoclub.org) and CD-ROM.

Does it do any good? Evidently it does. A study conducted by the University of California at Berkeley concluded that kids who have listened to Otto remember safety messages much better than those who haven't.

California State Automobile Association
Traffic Safety Department
150 Van Ness Ave., San Francisco, CA 94102
(415) 565-2310

Illustration by Teressa Cannata, St. Brendan's School, San Francisco, CA. Adapted from her award-winning poster in the 50th National Traffic Safety Poster Program 1994.
© 1994 California State Automobile Association

California State Automobile Association

LEFT: Safety poster contest winner, 1994.

TOP: Safety poster from *Motorland* magazine, April 1950.

ABOVE: Safety patroller, 1957.

At the very dawn of the automotive age, as the unconfirmed tale is told, there were but two cars, both in the same city. Might have been St. Louis. They ran into each other: The need for traffic safety was born.

SAFETY FIRST

CSAA has recognized this need from the very beginning, and its efforts in this regard have been many and varied. One of the most compelling is the sponsorship of traffic safety patrols at schools throughout northern California, Nevada, and Utah.

You have seen them: kids with sweaters or sashes or armbands, sometimes caps, occasionally semaphores, stopping traffic temporarily and escorting their classmates across busy intersections. It teaches children to be extra careful when they are walking. It also saves lives.

In San Francisco the school safety patrols began in the early 1920s, a joint project of the police, the schools, and CSAA. By 1929, the *San Francisco Chronicle* could report that eighteen thousand young traffic wardens had massed in front of City Hall to cheer as four of their number received commendations for saving the life of one of their fellow students during the previous year. The awards were presented by Chief of Police William J. Quinn and CSAA Public Safety Committee Chairman Percy E. Towne. The awards ceremony has continued with much pomp and ceremony to this day.

Today, the program is run in conjunction with national AAA, which recognizes patrollers who save a life while on duty. In the fifty years since the award has been national (recipients win a medal and a trip to the White House or to AAA headquarters in Florida), no fewer than ten have come from CSAA's service area.

LEFT: From "Sniffing Out Drunk Drivers," artwork by John Cuneo, *Motorland* magazine November/December 1996.

BELOW: CSAA's "Cheers!" non-alcoholic beverage pamphlet, 1999.

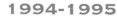
1994

● A 6.7 magnitude earthquake centered in Northridge, California, strikes the Los Angeles basin killing 57 people and causing $10 billion in damage.

● A.A.A. Utah becomes part of the C.S.A.A. family of states, which include California and Nevada.

● C.S.A.A. offers travel discounts to W.W.II veterans returning to Europe on the fiftieth anniversary of D-Day.

● In a sign of the times, carjacking and drive-by shootings are now considered a new category of felony.

1995

● Floods during this year will create the largest number of claims for one catastrophic event for C.S.A.A.: 1,800 auto claims and 10,000 homeowner's claims.

● C.S.A.A. initiates A.A.A. Plus service for members.

● Otto the Auto is kidnapped! Otto the Auto (C.S.A.A.'s remote-controlled traffic safety educator mini-car) disappears when the van he is stored in is stolen from C.S.A.A.'s main office in San Francisco. A frantic search ensues and Otto is recovered. Like many car theft victims, however, he has been plundered for parts and will require extensive rebuilding.

● The new Antioch District Office of C.S.A.A. is deemed the most energy efficient commercial building in the U.S.

A problem that has plagued the motorist—and therefore been a major concern of CSAA for many years—has been the lethal combination of driving and alcohol. An investigation by *Motorland* in 1980 revealed that, on any given night on any given California highway, one in ten drivers is under the influence. The carnage is horrible, costing thousands of lives and millions of dollars in damage each year. CSAA has been a staunch supporter of programs and laws to combat drunk driving for much of its existence. One clever program it runs is the "Cheers" guide, which offers recipes for nonalcoholic drinks to encourage safe entertaining.

ADDY Award Winner

Cheers!
Liquor-less libations to make your party swing

A long-running preoccupation of CSAA has been safety, especially the safety of teen drivers. As any parent will confirm, sending a child out onto the roads and highways is a terrifying prospect, especially in light of the sobering statistics on teens and drunk driving. As of the mid-1990s, traffic crashes killed more teenagers than anything else; approximately one-third of kids between fifteen and twenty who died, died in crashes, many more than died from gunshots, drugs, or any other cause.

There are many reasons for this awful fact. One is that driver training has declined over the years owing to lack of funds, despite the best efforts of AAA and other responsible agencies. Driver education—instruction in how a car's engine works, introduction to rules and laws—has long been offered to all high-school students. Driver training—behind-the-wheel instruction—used to be offered, free, to all students. But in the early '90s, state funds for behind-the-wheel training were cut, and many schools dropped their driver training programs. By the mid-1990s, many students had to pay hundreds of dollars for driver's ed and driver's training to become licensed before they turned eighteen. To address the problem, AAA made teen driver education and licensing a top national priority,

RIGHT: *VIA* magazine illustration, 1999.

BELOW: Teach Your Teen to Drive, AAA video ad, 1997.

Now you can start teaching your teen to drive without even starting the car.

Teaching your teen to drive? Before reaching for the keys, reach for AAA's safe driving program. It comes with an easy-to-follow 50-minute video and written lesson plan designed for you and your new driver. It'll help you teach your teen safe driving habits, all from the comfort of your favorite couch. And it's available at a Members-only price of just $21.95.* To order, call 1-800-327-3444 and mention number 9900.

RED-LIGHT RUNNING

BY LISA KLUBER

A PUBLIC MENACE

supporting improved driver training and graduated licensing laws. California's AAA clubs led the fight for this new approach to licensing in California and, as of July 1, 1999, before they can take the license test, California teens must log fifty hours behind the wheel (ten of them at night) in the company of a licensed adult. A similar law adopted in Florida was at least partly responsible for a drop in the teenage collision rate there. Everyone hopes the news in California is at least as good.

To help parents do their part, the association produced an elaborate package called "Teaching Your Teen to Drive." It included a handbook, video, and CD-ROM.

Another dreadful problem the association has lent a hand toward solving is that of red-light running. According to an article in *VIA*, fully one-fifth of the people killed in traffic accidents in 1995 nationwide—eight thousand out of forty thousand—perished because drivers disregarded traffic signals or, worse, took a yellow light as an invitation to speed up rather than slow down. This is a problem still far from being solved, but at least it is getting some of the attention it deserves.

ABOVE: CSAA used children's art to make its point in an anti-red-light running ad campaign.

Emergency Road Service Rides the Air Waves

ABOVE: The club made it easier to get emergency road service by offering cell phones with one-touch ERS access.

RIGHT: Otto the Auto safety ad with Marlo Thomas, 1993.

BELOW: *Motorland* magazine poll, 1946.

California State Automobile Association and CSAA Inter-Insurance Bureau

During this same period, CSAA also expanded its service into Utah, began offering life insurance to its members, joined the throng on the Internet (a natural for all the services CSAA offers), issued its own credit card, upgraded the technology that ensures a tow truck will reach a stranded motorist as quickly as possible, retooled its claims department, and began sending Otto the Auto to schools to teach children about auto safety years before they climb behind the wheel. (Lest this all sound too ideal, let us confess that *Motorland* confidently announced in 1980 that by July of 1981 all gasoline in California would be sold by the liter. Nobody is perfect.)

When it comes to upgrading cars with the latest improvements, CSAA has always been eager to help its members. In 1946, *Motorland* polled it readers, asking "What do you want in your post-war car?" understanding that "...in most cases these amenities would add to the cost." Respondents could vote for a defroster for the windshield, rear-window wiper, turn signals, visible gauge for engine oil level, all doors hinged at front, lock on gas tank, single key for ignition and door, air conditioning, radio, automatic transmission, and so forth—things we take utterly for granted a half-century later.

154

Today CSAA experts are helping plan for the car of the future, with features that seem fanciful and futuristic but may well be, in fact, right around the corner, limited mainly by cost. Among them:

- A tiny gadget that will immediately telephone 911 if you get into an accident telling whoever answers the precise location of your car

- A computer with satellite uplink that will tell you how much fuel you have in your tank, the distance to the closest open gas station, and the price the station is charging for various grades of fuel

- A highway with magnetic gadgets imbedded in the roadway to steer the car for you

- A computer-controlled system whereby cars could travel on the highway at today's speed limits, or faster, only inches apart and in complete safety, thus virtually eliminating congestion

TOP: The club's Web site ad ran in January/February 1997. The connection between a giant prairie dog and the Web is in the mind of the beholder.

NEW VISIONS, NEW DIRECTIONS

RIGHT: The new direction might be summed up as onward and upward.

The very first service CSAA offered to members was, appropriately enough, a map. The map was followed in rapid succession by a host of other auto-related services, some of which remain central to AAA members today, and some of which—like the combination radiator-stopper-CSAA emblem—have gone the way of the Stanley Steamer.

While public service—good roads, just laws, and matters pertaining to safety—was critical to CSAA's mission from its founding, service to members was the young organization's other leading priority. "The member comes first," said general manager Dave Watkins in CSAA's first official publication, and for Watkins and his staff, that meant always looking for new needs to meet and new ways to meet them.

for auto insurance, eurail passes, passport photos, and new maps. The club magazine expanded to a full-size, four-color format, and high-limit accident coverage was introduced, as were homeowners and personal liability insurance coverage. Members could have their cars evaluated at a CSAA facility and repaired at a CSAA-approved shop, where technicians were trained by CSAA. They could buy a car with pre-negotiated pricing or order a full packet of information about a vehicle's pricing, performance, and safety record.

At one time, members could even buy tires and batteries directly from CSAA's Club Tire and Battery program, but eventually, inventory challenges overwhelmed the value, and the service was discontinued. Film developing suffered a similar fate.

As the twentieth century drew to a close, members found the development of new members services and new ways to access them continued. Discounts on everything from truck rentals to eyeglasses were available through the Show Your Card & Save program, and AAA Worldwide Travel service negotiated special member benefits and prices from the world's leading travel suppliers. CSAA introduced a credit card, life insurance, and other financial services. And reflecting a century-long commitment to meeting members' auto needs, it also opened AAA Car Care Plus to provide the very best in auto repair from a name members could trust.

Looking to the future, CSAA is developing new services that will bring telecommunications technology to the traveler in new and exciting ways. When future members need to know where to go, where to stay, what to do, AAA will put the very best, most relevant information on their desktop, their dashboard—or in the palm of their hands.

SERVICES

In the teens and 1920s, CSAA recommended garages and hotels, helped members find the best way to get where they wanted to go, provided maps and other written material to travelers—and posted the official road signs on all northern California roads, helped write the nation's most comprehensive motor vehicle code, launched a transportation financing system still in use today, and formed some of the nation's first school safety patrols.

CSAA also began two of its longest-running and most popular services—auto insurance from the not-for-profit CSAA Inter-Insurance Bureau in 1914 and Emergency Road Service in 1924.

Following World War II, California began an explosive period of growth—and this was matched by explosive growth in services offered to members: Auto financing, lifetime renewal

As the association enters its second century it is constantly searching for ways to be more useful to its members. As an example, the Internet is poised to change travel planning forever: anyone can go online and compile a stupefying amount of information on resorts, cruises, hotels, transportation options, restaurants, car-rental companies, and so forth. The information is free, more or less, but it is provided by the seller and therefore not always trustworthy. AAA's Website, by contrast, evaluates all such items before recommending them, thus potentially saving members a great deal of time and helping them avoid costly mistakes.

When those twenty-five visionaries met at the Cliff House in 1900 to give birth to an auto club, the future was full of promise. Over the ensuing century, AAA became synonymous with fair-priced auto insurance, excellent road maps, tow trucks and roadside service, vacation planning, safety programs, and much, much more.

A hundred years later, the future still holds promise and mystery. No one can say with certainty what our world will look like in the next century, but there is one thing we can be sure of, and that is CSAA's commitment to the safety, security, and peace of mind of its members.

This distinctive emblem has been created

IN RECOGNITION OF CSAA'S LONG-TERM MEMBERS

Members who supported the CSAA over the years contributed significantly to the growth of our organization. Their loyalty is an important factor in the Association's ability to expand services and benefits that all members now enjoy.

As an expression of our appreciation, members enrolled for twenty-five years or more may receive this special emblem. Two versions are available, a bumper sticker and a windshield decal. If you wish, you may have both.

How to Get Your Free Emblem.

If you're eligible, you can pick up your emblem at any CSAA office. If it is more convenient, you can request the emblem by mail. Mail your request to: California State Automobile Association, Membership Records, P.O. Box 11100, San Francisco, CA 94101.

Please tell us if you want a bumper sticker, windshield emblem or both. If you own more than one automobile, we'll be happy to enclose additional emblems.

We are proud of your continued support and hope you'll be proud to display this token of appreciation.

PRESIDENT

ABOVE: Membership recognition, March 1983.

BELOW: This Dr. Seuss cartoon from the 1940s envisioned a carpooling system slightly more ambitious than the one we have today.

Index

Page references in *italicized* type refer to illustrative material; those in **boldface** type refer to sidebars.

Produced by Welcome Enterprises for VIA Books, a division of California State Automobile Association, 150 Van Ness Avenue, San Francisco, California 94102. All rights reserved.

www.aaa.com

Welcome Enterprises
588 Broadway, Suite 303
New York, N.Y. 10012
(212) 343-9430 Fax (212) 343-9434

Project Director: Lena Tabori
Project Editor: Natasha Tabori Fried
Designer: Jon Glick

Printed in Singapore

Library of Congress
Cataloging-in-Publication Data
On file by request
ISBN 0-941807-42-8

FIRST EDITION
2 4 6 8 10 9 7 5 3 1

Dedicated to the members of CSAA, who helped turn a dream into a great 20th century success story.
—Don Patton,
Vice President/Publishing
CSAA

A FEW THANKS FROM WELCOME:

To Don Patton, for his editorial guidance, unflagging enthusiasm and support for the breadth and magnitude of this project; to Peter Beren, for assembling the team and for asking us in late September 1999 to do the impossible and then remaining confident, through rocky times, that we would deliver this book as promised; to Tom Turner and John Sparks, who delivered the text, both interesting and on time; to John Goepel, whose deliciously eccentric persona could never hide his wealth of knowledge and talent; to Alison Moore, who brought commitment and dedication to her myriad of contributions; to her assistants Penny Ahlstrand and Josh Ragent, to Richard Berkvam, Marvin Parker, who worked with Alison to photograph the CSAA archive; to Tom and Jean Moulin, whose photography collection of three generations of Moulin photographs (from 1884) were to be a source of endless fascination; to Galen and Barbara Rowell, for their generosity and their passion for California's wilderness and natural beauty; to Barry Sundermeier from their Mountain Light Studio, who made every dialogue a joy; to Bonnie Muench, wife of David—another great California photographer—who turned on a dime for us; to Janet Vail, who stepped in at the last minute and peacefully found the missing images still needed; and, finally, to those at CSAA who worked so kindly to make our job an easier one: Fatima Bucsit, the great and gentle facilitator; Merry Banks of Traffic Safety, Ron Evans of VIA, Jeff Holman in Cartography, Christopher Yains and Manjot Kochar in Marketing, and Molly White, able steward of the CSAA Centennial.

And, at Welcome, to Natasha Tabori Fried, our project editor, who saw the forest and the trees at all times. Always available, always enthusiastic, always focused on finding the best and doing the best, she watched over every detail. To Jon Glick, our designer, whose love of the material shows through on every page. He created a template of running text, sidebars, captions, and chron bars that allowed the material to organize itself as wonderfully as it has. And then, he embellished it.

And, finally, to Arthur Quek at Tien Wah Press, who saved us from ourselves.

—Lena Tabori,
President & Publisher

PHOTOGRAPHY CREDITS:

Cover/Pages 6, 8-9, 30-31, 66-67, 94-95, 120-121, 138-139, 143: © Galen Rowell/Mountain Light
Page 133: © David Muench
Back Cover (background image)/Pages 1, 4, 6, 10 (bottom), 12, 13, 16 (top & bottom), 17 (bottom), 19, 20-21, 22, 24 (top), 26-27, 38-39, 77 (all), 78-79, 80 (top), 81, 82-83, 84, 93, 95, 98-99, 113: © Moulin Archives San Francisco
Pages 69, 100 (top), 118 (bottom right), 119, 131 (top), 140 (top left), 140 (top right): © Corbis
All remaining images and materials courtesy of The California State Automobile Association Archives

Every attempt has been made to obtain permission to reproduce materials protected by copyright. Where omissions may have occurred, the producers will be happy to acknowledge this is future printings.